MODEL MARINE STEAM

MODEL MARINE STEAM

By Stan Bray

SPECIAL INTEREST MODEL BOOKS

Special Interest Model Books Ltd.
P.O. Box 327
Poole
Dorset
BH15 2RG

First published in 2006
Reprinted with corrections 2016
Reprinted 2021

ISBN 978-185486-245-6

Printed in Malta by Melita Press

Contents

Acknowledgements

I must confess that while I find model boating of great interest my real love is the steam engine and I would not even attempt to try and estimate how many I have built during a lifetime of model engineering. For many years I was involved in the running of workshops at modelling holidays and a very large part of the time was spent repairing, adjusting and even building steam plants for boats, not to mention the numerous time there was hull damage to be repaired. The number of tasks that we had to carry out on either the opening day or even the day before made it obvious that that many people were bringing in steam plants to be worked on for the simple reason that they had no knowledge of how to sort them out for themselves and yet so many were keen to operate steam boats. The interest was not limited to those with who had boats but also there were many that would like to own one but did not know how to start. From this situation of long ago came the realisation that many would like somewhere to turn for help and a book seemed the obvious answer.

Don Gordon I had known for many years, we used to visit the watchmakers' stall in Leather Lane in London, where cheap goodies such as wire drills were cheaply available and Don would invariably discuss his love of steam boats and his ideas on making scale rather than oversize steam plants. An amazing man he only ever used a treadle operated lathe, which he always maintained gave him better control than an electrically powered one and he made his point by producing exquisite models with it. Sadly Don passed away some years ago but I still have his original sketches and have relied heavily on his words of wisdom.

A chance meeting at an exhibition with Malcolm Beak, who I had never met before, resulted in him sending me the very next day a large quantity of material much of which I have used and I am most grateful to him for allowing me to do so.

Another old friend Chris Leggo and inveterate experimenter from the United States was also quick to help out once he knew what was happening.

John Thompson a model boating enthusiast was kind enough to invite me to his home to obtain some necessary material and he to has my heartiest thanks.

Roy Amsbury the designer of an electronic water level indicator, it was not intended for use in boats but after some discussion was tried and found to be a success and ultimately fitted with a small relay that operated a pump. Roy, who I also classed as a close friend, too unfortunately died before he could realise the full potential of his design.

Finally I must thank my wife who suffers in silence while I spend hours doing drawings and typing copy and then cheerfully and diligently checks my work for me, she is ultimately the one who makes this book possible.

Stan Bray January 2006

Introduction

Using steam power to drive model boats is almost as old as the use of steam to drive full sized vessels. A browse through model catalogues of the period around 1906 - 1910 shows a considerable variety of such boats for sale as complete models, in addition to numerous parts that were sold for the enthusiast wishing to make his own steam boat. These ranged from hulls made of either metal or wood, to parts with which to build the engine, including completed boilers. Most were fairly primitive in comparison with the models we see today, but even so they proved very popular and people in those days tended to be far less discerning regarding the authenticity of a model and more often than not were content to use their imagination. Even so there were at that time a number of high class model makers producing steam powered ships of realistic appearance, although more often than not the proportions of the steam plant left a great deal to be desired.

With more sophisticated tools and material available the modern model maker as a rule looks for a far greater degree of realism, in general this has been the trend not only in steamboats but also in model making as a whole. Modern technical developments have played

a very large part in this, in particular there is a far greater availability of good quality completed parts and accessories, in addition there is now a much more ready availability of machines to aid the model maker. The range of kits alone has become vast and there are many more prototypes now for which kits are available. Much of the machinery currently available was unheard of as far as the modeller was concerned and all these facts have resulted in the steady improvement we now see. In spite of this a great many home made steam plants are still of primitive construction, badly designed and oversized and it is hoped that this book will go some way to redressing these matters.

The Unimat 4 one of many small lathes now available for the dedicated model maker.

A small milling machine by Unimat, whilst not a necessity for building small steam plants it is a desirable luxury that some years ago would not have been possible to buy.

The photograph opposite shows a typical model that is available commercially, the boat and complete steam plant are of a type that can be purchased from a number of sources.

In full sized practice we can generally say that the means of driving a boat has gone through four stages. We can lump together manpower and sail, as for many years they went hand in hand, there were many ancient ships that were powered by oarsmen alone and others that also had sails. If we forget those very early vessels, for many years sail alone was used as the method for propelling ships, for whatever purpose they were used.

The invention of the steam engine was to change all that and as soon as a satisfactory method of fitting a steam plant was discovered, the change from sail to steam was inevitable. Although in spite of the efficiency of steam, sail was still used for many years, sometimes on its own and on other occasions as an auxiliary to the steam engine. There was also a change in the means of the application of steam, early ships having paddle wheels and later ones driven by propellers. The story of these changes is in itself a history worth studying but it is not the purpose of this book to relate the facts in detail.

There were many disadvantages to reciprocating steam engine propulsion, and as the internal combustion engine gradually succeeded in other forms of transport, it again became inevitable that there would be a change in the marine world; the steam engine was gradually phased out, but not without a fight. It did not and has not died completely as many ships, particularly large ones, are driven by turbines and these are of course steam engines. They work on a rotary rather than reciprocating system but nevertheless are still driven by steam.

The operation of a turbine has little relationship to that of the reciprocating engine and the methods of providing steam have also changed. It used to be coal fired boilers that were used and this meant that men earned their living by putting coal on fires all day. Tons and tons of it would be needed and as the boilers were in the bowels of the ship it was a nasty unpleasant task, calling for great physical effort. The boilers are now mainly heated by burning oil, or in some cases even via a nuclear reactor, no physical effort is required and life for the stoker is now a very pleasant proposition indeed. The vast quantities of coal that had to be stored in order to keep the boilers going also used valuable space in the ship and it is not surprising therefore that the change to liquid fuel was rapidly made.

In the world of model boats there are four choices of power supply. The use of sail is very popular and has a huge following, considerable skill is required to operate a boat under sail and it is therefore not surprising that sailing boats are very popular. The use of internal combustion engines has met with a rather mixed response and to some degree this is not the fault of the model makers. Many local authorities will not allow boats powered by internal combustion engines to be used on water under their control, because allegedly the noise disturbs other people in the area as well as the wild life and there is frequently pollution associated with the engines. This has met with a rather mixed reception amongst model makers and there are still many die-hards who will travel a considerable distance to use boats powered by internal combustion engines, particularly for racing.

The electric motor has found great favour, it is cheap to buy, easy to fit into a boat and simple to operate, and almost silent in operation, what more could one ask for? In many ways therefore electric motors are ideal, but somehow they lack life and do not have that touch of excitement that other means of propulsion do. Even so most model makers will without doubt continue to use them because they are so convenient and cheap and if it gets people into the hobby that is fine. In addition the very silence associated with electric propulsion does not find favour with everyone and there are units available to make the appropriate noise that is missing.

Where does all this leave steam power? Well it is generally much more dirty, it can be difficult to fit some steam plants into boats and it is not always as reliable as it might be, although the latter depends to a large degree on the ability of the operator. So much for the down side, but when we come to the plus there is little doubt that a steam driven boat has its own fascination and is alive with the steam plant being part of the boat, rather than an add on designed just to provide power. The steam boat always attracts the attention of onlookers because of this. Observe an owner preparing his or her boat and there will invariably be people watching to see what is going on and asking questions about the steam plant, and many will stand and watch the boat put through its paces, there is an air of excitement as it does so.

For a large proportion of people the steam engine

is a mystery and that is why the easier option is taken, it is hoped that this book will unravel many or perhaps all of those mysteries and encourage readers to have a go at steam operation. Making a steam engine is well within the capabilities of most people and doing so gives a lot of satisfaction.

There are many steam plants that can be bought and if that is what one wishes to do so be it, however the main intention here is to encourage readers to make their own steam engines and so add greatly to the fun of model making. Although a simple steam plant can be made, using nothing more than hand tools, it must be said it generally requires the use of a small lathe, such machines are now available quite cheaply and if no workshop is available they can be put away after use. As pure metalworking skills are no longer taught in schools it might be that people are put off by the thought that a great deal of skill is needed. This is not so and there are numerous books available that describe how to use a lathe, they can either be bought or borrowed from the local library. It takes no time at all to master the basics for using a machine and as many steam engines are very simple things a steam plant can be made in a very short period of time.

1
Steam Plant Design

There is a certain fascination about steam and the machines it drives, invariably a steam driven locomotive, motorcar, boat or stationary engine will attract attention when it is working. This is reflected in the number of people who go to steam themed events and this interest also passes into the field of model boating. A well-made model boat, powered by electric motors will always look good and attract a certain number of interested spectators. A boat powered by a steam engine does however attract more, even if the vessel is not such a good model as the electric powered one. If for some reason or reasons the steam plant does not function very well and possibly the operator has to keep making adjustments that do not always work, many of the onlookers will soon drift away. We must face the fact that many steam plants in boats are temperamental and almost inevitably this is caused by bad design or bad manufacture, or perhaps even a little of both.

In addition to bad manufacture a common problem is that the steam plant, or maybe only parts of it are not really suited to the vessel in which they are housed. Perhaps the most common thing is that all too often we see boats that are powered by engines and boilers that are far too large. (A theme that will be continually returned to throughout this book). A common feature for many years, which is now hopefully on the decline was to fit twin cylinder engines with cylinder bores of ¾in or 20mm or so, in a model of an open launch about three feet or a metre in length. Include the large boiler necessary to supply an engine of that size with steam and there will be very little room left for anything else, so the first thing

Although a very nice model to build, this Stuart twin is far too big for the average model boat, most require an engine of less than half the size.

to consider is making or if necessary purchasing engines and boilers of scale proportions. If the engine and boiler are well made the boat will most certainly work, but will never look like a real launch, because the steam plant is so out of scale.

If we think of the open launch as a start and there were many of them years ago and quite a few of them it is pleasing to know are still in existence now, the boiler would be housed roughly amidships. There would then be ample room for the occupants of the boat to walk around it; more often than not there would be seats alongside it with plenty of legroom for passengers. This means that with a beam of say five inches or a hundred and twenty

A single cylinder oscillating engine like this can be used to power a small boat but starting and reversing it remotely is difficult, therefore a two cylinder engine is advisable.

five millimetres, the boiler should be no more than two and a half inches or say sixty-five millimetres in diameter. Perhaps in the interests of getting the best from the boat that figure could be stretched to three inches or seventy five millimetres, but anything larger will be vastly out of proportion.

Let us also look at the type of engine referred to above, 3/4in bore cylinders are absolutely ludicrous. Model engineers who make steam locomotives that haul passengers frequently use engines of that size on their models and the locomotive will happily haul half a dozen people. Don't forget that in addition to the weight of the people it will have to cope with the friction of the wheels on the rails as well as that of a couple of passenger wagons. All that the engine has to do in a boat is to push aside the water and carry its own weight, which is nowhere near that of a model locomotive. Model traction engine enthusiasts will also use that size of cylinder on a two-inch scale model traction engine. Here there is even more friction to be overcome and only a single cylinder will be used, so it really just does not make sense to use such a large set up in a model boat.

It is not only launches that can be powered by steam, it is also applicable to many other types of ship and yet only rarely do we see anything other than the odd tug that is so powered. There is no doubt two reasons for this: the first is the fact that people are trying to use vastly oversized steam plants, secondly the superstructure has to be removed in order to get at the plant. The first is easily overcome, simply make the unit more in proportion. The second is of course a necessity, but with the use of a smaller and more efficient plant, the problem is reduced, for example instead of a vertical format for the engine, why not a horizontal one? More room will make it a lot easier to use a superstructure that is easier to take off in order to deal with any problems that might arise.

Power in relation to design

How much power a steam engine transmits will depend on numerous design factors, for example an oscillating engine, no matter how well made will be unlikely to give the same power as one fitted with slide or piston valves, even if the workmanship on the latter is of a lower standard than that on the oscillating engine. Having said that, it in no way infers that oscillating engines are unsatisfactory, far from it, after all they were used in full sized practice for many years with considerable success. Accepting that generally speaking a slide or piston valve engine will be more efficient that the oscillator, this does not mean that if the latter is used it must be vastly over scale and we must also accept the fact that many readers will have neither the equipment or expertise to build the more complicated type. Expertise is something that comes with practice and so there is no reason why those with little or no knowledge of metalworking techniques should not be able to eventually build the engine of their dreams.

Single or multiple cylinders?

The power transmitted will ultimately depend not only on the type of engine but as we would expect also on the size of the cylinder or cylinders. There is very little difference in cylinder capacity, if we take a single cylinder of a particular size, or two cylinders of approximately half the size of the single. But we can expect the two-cylinder engine to provide more power than the single cylinder one, merely because of the more continuous thrust and so the conclusion must be that where possible an engine with multiple cylinders should be used. In addition a multiple cylinder engine will always be a great deal easier to start than a single cylinder one.

Friction

No matter how well made an engine is there is certain to be loss as a result of friction, but with modern materials it is possible to reduce this considerably. Tiny ball races can be used instead of plain bearings. and while initially these may feel stiff once they have been used for a while and freed up, the reduction in friction is quite amazing. Modern materials can also assist; for example where it is possible substitute a metal to metal surface with a set up where one of the surfaces is made of PTFE, there can again be a considerable improvement in efficiency. Teflon is another plastic worth considering as a means of increasing efficiency and these plastics also reduce heat loss, another cause of reduced power.

Heat loss

A major cause of power reduction is heat loss and this is often caused through not giving it enough consideration during the design stage. For example if a cylinder is made from a length of ½ in or 12mm diameter brass and bored 3/8 in or 10mm, the wall thickness of 1/16in or 1mm is absorbing heat and then releasing it to the atmosphere. By simply reducing the wall thickness to approximately 50% can increase the efficiency of the engine by a considerable amount. If in addition to that some form of lagging can be applied the heat loss is reduced even more. Reduction of heat loss in this fashion means that the boiler can operate more efficiently and so not only do we get an increase in power but in all probability also an extended running time on a boiler filling.

Other contributing factors

There are other factors that can contribute to reducing efficiency, if the alignment between the engine and propeller is slightly out this can cause a certain amount of drag and stop the full power being used. Some people like to connect to the final drive via gears, but it is worth mentioning that gears always cause loss of power because of the friction they create and so if they are used it is important to ensure they are properly meshed. Badly adjusted gears can cause a large power loss. In the case of a single cylinder engine the size and weight of the flywheel is very important, the heavier the flywheel is, the greater the power it will store and then return to the engine. A multi-cylinder engine will work without a flywheel but as a rule fitting one will improve the running qualities. While the fact that flywheels are beneficial is not in doubt, if they are too large and heavy they have a reverse effect and actually absorb some of the power of the engine. It is always worthwhile experimenting to try and discover what size of flywheel is best suited to the engine.

Boilers

Boiler construction is dealt with in detail at a later stage, but it is worth mentioning in relation to power, that in order for an engine to be efficient it must be supplied with sufficient steam. Developments in the field of boiler making and in particular methods of heating mean that it is possible for the boiler to be a great deal more efficient than our forbears would have dreamed possible.

Making the boat

Numerous books have been written about building model boats and the author does not wish to be considered little more than a novice when it comes to methods of construction. However one aspect of boat building that is pertinent to this book is that of the materials to use when the boat is made. There is no doubt that by far the greater percentage of model boats is now made from kits, of which there are now hundreds available. The vast majority of these kits is designed for use with electric motors and is completely unsuitable for use with a steam plant.

The increasing use of vacuum formed plastic superstructure and now in many cases hulls as well, severely limits the use of kit built boats.

The boats made in this way look superb and are comparatively easy to construct but the materials are not generally suitable for being steam powered. Vacuum forming is done by heating the plastic, so that the plastic sheet has been made flexible, then removing the air from underneath and allowing air pressure on top to press the plastic over a suitable mould. (It is a simple process that can be done at home with the use of a vacuum cleaner and with thin plastic, nothing more than a kettle of hot water is needed to make it flexible.) The heat required therefore is less than that generated by a steam plant so in all probability that lovely superstructure will end up moulded to the shape of the engine and boiler. No doubt this would make a nice dummy set up for the next boat that should be steam powered but would be driven by electricity, it is not exactly what we are aiming for. In the case of a plastic formed hull, in no time at all it is possible that the precious steam plant would have to be retrieved from the bottom of the pond. Therefore the materials used must be able to withstand a certain degree of heat and possibly the best of these, if we disregard metal is wood. Metal has of course been successfully used, but making a boat in steel or aluminium will surely be beyond the capability of most. GRP or glass fibre as it is generally known will withstand the amount of heat we are talking about and can be considered as suitable for anyone wishing for a pre-formed hull and there are a number of kits with hulls that are made from it. The traditional wooden boat is very suitable indeed, as wood is an excellent insulator, it is the material most commonly used by the scratch builder and there are still many kits that use it.

The size of the steam plant should be carefully chosen in relation to that of the hull, a good supply of air is essential to keep burners working properly and this must be reflected in the relationship between the sizes of hull and steam plant, particularly if there is a superstructure. The steam plant should be mounted on a metal plate so that it can be withdrawn as easily as possible and

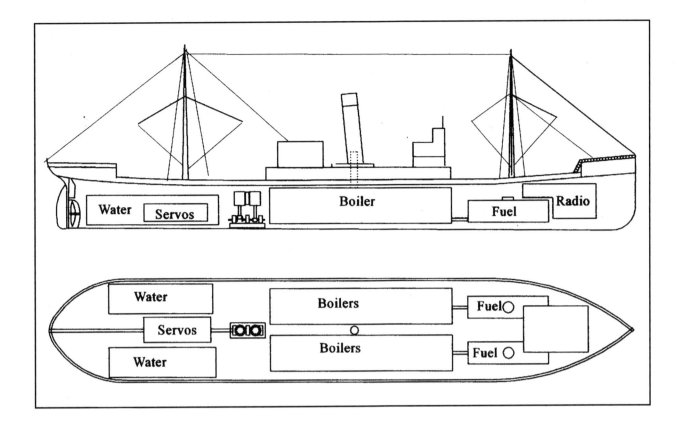

it is advisable to have a small lip to the plate just in case of fuel spillage. If it is not possible to make this right around the whole steam plant, then at least set the fuel tank in some form of recessed tray so that if fuel does spill it will not spread into the boat where is could catch fire and cause irreparable damage.

Adequate provision for exhaust is essential and there are two types to contend with. There is the exhaust from the engine that will be in the form of wet steam that if it cannot escape will in no time at all drench the boat in water and there is the heat exhaust from the boiler. In full size practice the steam exhaust is used to draw the fires and keep them hot, a special valve known as the blower would be fitted to assist the process when pressure got a little low. Unless the boiler is coal fired this does not apply so much in model form, nevertheless the addition of the exhaust from the engine will help to keep a good air supply to the burner and unless it is

impractical to do so, the steam should be exhausted together with the excess heat from the burner.

Location of engines

The location of the power plant is most important and as far as possible it should usually be placed as near the centre of the boat as practical, this will assist in trimming. In particular the position of the boiler should be carefully selected. It is worth remembering that there will be turbulence created by the water being heated in the boiler, not to mention the fact that it will slop about with the movement of the boat and therefore the more central it is the better the stability. Most full sized ships used in the steam age had the engine and the boiler in particular placed centrally. The modern trend on cargo boats is to situate the boiler towards the stern; it is there now that we see the funnel, which these days is usually only a glorified exhaust pipe. This is because the heavy

Suggested engine and boiler layout for a coaster. There should be 4 water tanks (2 at each side) leaving room for the propeller shaft to go between them in the stern.

machinery and large boilers are no longer used and by locating the superstructure there, more room is left for deck cargo and hatches.

In model steamboats it is usual to set the engine behind the boiler, nearer to the stern, which allows a shorter arrangement for the transmission. If the boiler is set towards the stern it will be necessary for the distribution of weight to put the engine amidships and we then run into problems with the situation of the propeller shaft. If the design of the boat is such that it is deemed necessary to have the engine in front of the boiler then the arrangements for supporting the boiler will need to take this into account. The connecting arrangement between engine and propeller can then be designed to pass underneath. In these circumstances thought must also be given to the type of boiler used. The height required for a pot boiler with water tubes below could well be prohibitive and so a boiler based on the Scotch Type principle or a multi-barrelled type will be the best type to use.

Weight distribution is most important and all boating enthusiasts will know only too well that the last thing needed is for the boat to become top heavy. The question of engine size is discussed elsewhere, no matter how small we can make the engine if the cylinders are at the top they are the heaviest part and will be at the highest point. Marine engineers were of course quite aware of this and particularly on older ships, solved the problem by turning the engine more or less upside down, thus keeping the weight at the bottom. This was particularly applicable to oscillating engines, where several tons of cast iron cylinder waving about in the air was most undesirable. In later years when triple expansion engines became common this was less practical and the engines were once again turned up the right way, however by then improvements in design meant that engines were generally more compact and the weight less of problem. The improvement in weight distribution was mainly achieved in the casting used for the cylinders, at first they were frequently solid, later the improvements available

in casting techniques allowing them to be cast in a different way.

Steam plants should always if possible be mounted complete on a metal tray, this ensures that they are easy to remove, there is little that is worse than having to disconnect the boiler from the heat source and engine in order to remove it for some maintenance to be carried out. All parts should be screwed firmly to the metal tray, which in turn should be firmly mounted in the hull. If possible it is best to devise some form of clip for one end and a screw down set up for the other.

Materials

It is possible to purchase a kit of parts for an engine and it is reasonable to assume that in that case the materials supplied will be suitable. Such kits come in a variety of forms, the most basic being little more than a set of castings with which to make the cylinders and port blocks and possibly material with which to make a suitable frame. The more sophisticated yet basic kit will include not only the casting referred to above, but also all other materials needed to finish the model, even including the screws. Then there is a the kit where the main machining has been completed and further advanced still, the type where all parts have been made and it is just a case of bolting the lot together.

Because of the amount of work involved in putting a kit together, at whatever level it will necessarily be rather expensive and for this reason as well as the pride in doing so, many people prefer to make their own engines from standard materials. In that case the correct selection of materials is important. There are differences of opinion as to whether the best material to use for cylinders is brass or bronze. This is because in the case of brass, which is an alloy that includes, copper and zinc, extended exposure to ordinary tap water at high temperature can cause the zinc content to leach away, leaving a powdery residue that has absolutely no use. While this can happen it takes

a very long time and also generally happens at higher temperatures than are likely to be used in model boats. Also the effect appears to take place in boiler fittings where the water line meets air, something that does not apply to an engine, so the use of brass should not be excluded. Temperature is directly related to pressure and the pressure needed to drive a boat is considerably lower than that which is frequently used.

Bronze is without doubt harder wearing than most brass, there is a whole range of brass and bronze alloy specifications and much will depend on the type of material chosen or available. Generally speaking unless a special free machining type is obtained, bronze will be more difficult to work with than brass. One must decide between the extra strength of bronze as against the ease of working in the case of brass. In general it is fair

to say that brass will be quite adequate for the cylinders of most engines.

Stainless steel should be used for such items as connecting rods and possibly the engine superstructure. It should also be used for pistons; it is never wise to use two identical materials as bearings surfaces mating with each other and so whether brass or bronze is used for the cylinders it is best to use stainless steel for the pistons in order to prevent excessive wear. The pivot should also be made from stainless steel, as mild steel is likely to rust in that position.

Mild steel can be used for crankshafts and bronze or brass for main and big end bearings, thus giving us the two dissimilar metals as bearing surfaces. Mild steel does rust quite easily and so it will be a case of keeping plenty of oil on it to prevent this happening. A good alternative to mild steel is silver steel, as it has a higher carbon content than

Steam plants need not be confined to open boats, as can be seen by this photograph of a steam trawler seen at the Kirklees Steam Convention.

(Photograph courtesy of Richard Simpson)

mild steel and is harder wearing, it is though just as prone to rust as mild steel and so the application of plenty of oil still applies.

Assuming that most people wish to purchase screws rather than make them, it will be best to use those made from stainless steel, they are available at the majority of model engineering suppliers and are less prone to rust than mild steel ones. Unless a really good grade is obtained, stainless steel will rust and so even with the use of stainless steel screws there is still a necessity to keep a check on possible corrosion. Brass will be suitable in some places but generally it is better avoided, as it is not unknown for the threads to seize making it impossible to remove them without breaking, should it be necessary to strip the engine down at any time. The person who makes his or her own screws will do well to consider using bronze, which answers all purposes.

All these points will make for an efficient and attractive looking steamboat and many happy hours sailing it.

2
Boiler Water

Something that is a constant concern to operators of model steam plants is whether or not the water used should be treated, a subject that seems to have no clear answer as opinions vary. The water companies in Britain and no doubt other countries as well all mix various chemicals with the water supply, and these vary from area to area. The result is that while one district has a water supply that is very hard and therefore creates a great deal of scale, others have a supply that is comparatively soft, there being little sign of scale forming. The chemicals are put in for a number of reasons, the obvious ones being to ensure there is no contamination that might be injurious to the health of people using it. One of the chemicals used is calcium and this is put in partly to purify the water, but most importantly to seal off leaks in main pipes that are many years old. It is therefore likely to be used more profusely in urban areas where there is a lot of old property.

Over a period of time joins in the pipes, particularly where fittings have been used start to leak and because they are buried, it is not easy to repair them, however the formation of scale inside the pipes acts as a sealant and saves the water company the necessity and cost of having to do so. We see evidence of this build up of scale in the home where it forms round the rim of taps and can be very difficult to remove. This scale

formation is even more evident in the kettle being accelerated by the boiling of the water. The idea of using such material to seal off the pipes is fine as far as the water companies are concerned but it has its disadvantage in the home as it assists the formation of scale in the domestic water system.

It follows therefore that if ordinary tap water is used in a model boiler scale will form and in some ways this is fine as if there are any small leaks around fittings over a period of time the scale acts as a filler and stops them. Unfortunately the scale also forms inside the boiler and adheres to the copper, there it will act as an insulator and over period of years the heat transfer from the boiler shell to the water will be reduced, resulting in bad steaming properties. It can also have another adverse effect, although this one is less likely, in as much as it seeps into any cracks or slightly open spaces in the boiler construction, as already described it acts as a sealer. However, during the course of time it will also cause the space to widen and in the event of treatment being carried out to remove the scale the cracks, or gaps will be larger than they were originally.

The use of distilled or deionised water will ensure that there is less if any at all furring up of the boiler, providing that only such water is ever used. If after a boiler has been used with distilled water for sometime, ordinary tap water is used, foaming occurs and this results in the boiler priming and throwing out its, contents via the engine exhaust. The same effect is likely to occur with a boiler regularly used with tap water and then on some particular occasion it is filled with distilled water.

Rain water

There is unlikely to be much calcium in rainwater and although these days it is slightly acid, clean rainwater can be very good. Collecting a suitable quantity is the problem, water that is drained from roofs contains all sorts of impurities and these are likely to cause priming. In addition it will usually contain a considerable amount of dirt so it must be filtered before use. Reports suggest mixed results from its use, in some cases it seems to be satisfactory and in others it is known to have caused priming. This may be the result of using it in boilers that have previously been filled with ordinary tap water, as there is no doubt that mixing water from different sources often does give problems. If rainwater is to be used it is probably best to start using it when the boiler is new and thereafter to use no other supply.

Pond water

Pond water is inevitably an unknown quantity, most ponds have a fair amount of dirt in them but most if not all will be free of calcium, providing the water can be well filtered it should be suitable and many owners of model boats use pond water with complete success. This means that it may well be possible to use a pump direct into the pond, rather than carrying an on board water supply. There is however a possibility that using pond water in a boiler previously regularly used with tap water might lead to priming.

Swimming baths

During modelling weeks at Holiday Camps and similar establishments it is not unusual for the swimming pool to be used for running model boats. The water should be free of foreign bodies but almost certainly will contain large quantities of calcium and therefore be unsuitable for use with a boiler that normally runs on rain or distilled water.

Water treatment

There are various water treatments available and one obvious answer is to use water that has been supplied through a domestic water softening system, this is best used within a short period of taking it from the tap as after a while it appears to lose its quality and we are more or less back to square one. The idea of using descaling treatments in the boiler during operation does not work too well either, descalers tend to create sludge in the water and this will result in the boiler priming. The use of sequestric acid works and a boiler examined after the water had been treated in this way over a period of months showed no sign at all of furring up. It is difficult material to get hold of and it is expensive.

Descaling

For most people the best answer will probably be to use either tap or rain water and to regularly descale the boiler, not necessarily after every use but certainly a couple or more times during a year. The process is simple enough, just put in a descaling solution, after the boiler has been blown down, leave it for a few days and then thoroughly wash the boiler out with cold water, making sure there is no residue. Ordinary vinegar makes a very effective descaling solution, although some people may prefer the use of a proprietary substance.

Blow down

All boilers should be regularly blown down in order to prevent the build up of unwanted deposits, blowing down consists of allowing pressure to drop to about 5psi and then opening a valve so that the remaining boiler contents are forced out under pressure. With this in mind it is always a good thing to include a blow down valve, if it is practical to do so, when making a boiler. When the contents of the boiler have been evacuated leave at least one valve open, more if possible and if the boiler has a

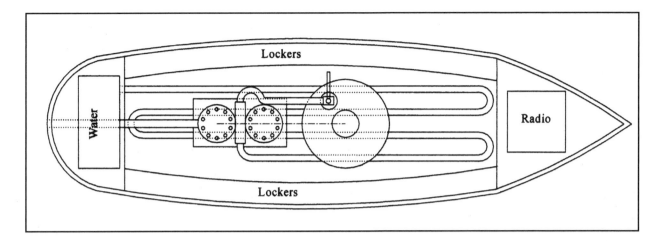

filler cap remove that, in order that it can be allowed to dry out thoroughly. If it is practical to do so the application of a little heat will also assist in the drying process.

De-zincification

The chemicals in modern water supplies are inclined to attack the zinc content of brass and the result can be pretty disastrous as the metal remaining turns to powder or sludge. The damage mainly appears around the water line at the position where there is considerable turbulence, but is not necessarily confined to that area. Therefore it is advisable that all fittings, such as stop cocks, regulators, etc should be made of bronze as should the bushes in which they are to be located and if fittings are purchased ensure they are of bronze, not brass.

Water supplies

How long a boat will remain in steam will depend on the amount of fuel and water that is available, if supplies can be replenished, without stopping the boat then it can remain on the water indefinitely. Of course we do not want it to do that, but it is nice when one can go for an afternoon sailing and not have to stop every ten minutes or so to replenish the water. Elsewhere there is information on how to maintain water levels and boiler

pressure, however it is no good knowing how to do that if there is not a ready water supply available with which the boiler can be replenished. This can be arranged fairly easily, unfortunately the same cannot be said for the fuel supply but as it takes far less room than the water there is no reason why sufficient fuel for a couple of hours cannot be made available.

The best way to economise on water is to run the engine on as low a pressure as possible; this is not to say that high pressure does not do the job, but that all too often high pressures are wasted. Also all steam joints should be kept in good order, not only do leaking joints waste steam but they will also spoil the appearance of the boat. They create condensation to which dirt and oil will adhere and once the steam has cooled it becomes very difficult to get the resultant mess off.

On-board supplies

Apart from economising on water, for lengthy periods of running additional supplies will be needed and while there might be nothing terribly wrong with using the water from the pond where the boat is being used, it will have to be very well filtered to prevent dirt from getting into the boiler. The impurities in pond water are likely to block the valves on

As many loops of condensing tubes as possible should be included of as small a diameter as practicable. By curving lengths of tubing and sealing the ends, additional water space is available in the lockers. As the condensing steam is still under pressure the tank must have a ventilation hole.

the pump and dirty water will cause priming. For those who have never experienced priming it is the effect of the steam being generated catching the water and literally throwing it out of the exhaust. The effect can be quite startling to anyone standing nearby and who suddenly finds himself or herself showered with hot water. Fortunately as a rule by the time the water has shot into the air and fallen back it will have cooled somewhat, so that while it is uncomfortable, there is not a great deal of chance that serious injury will be caused.

The best answer by far to the water supply situation is to have inboard tanks, which can usually be disguised in some way or another. For example a covered lifeboat makes an excellent water tank and for those building launches and similar vessels there is usually spare space in the lockers. If inboard water tanks are to be used then the next logical step is to re-circulate the engine exhaust, which after all is water.

It is essential if one is to do this that an oil separator is used, as oil and water do not mix, particularly under pressure in a boiler. It is also necessary to ensure that the tank to which the water is returned has sufficient ventilation. It is steam that is being returned to it and as we all know steam continues to expand until it finally condenses. Therefore if it is returned to a closed tank it is likely to build a fair amount of pressure and should the tank not be strong enough the result could well be that it will get damaged and the worst scenario of all could be that the tank will rupture under the pressure.

A simple condenser will help to cool the exhaust down and making one is not that difficult. One of the easiest ways of all to condense the steam is to put a series of loops of small-bore tubing along the keel, under the floorboards. Not only will the coils work as a condenser, but also in addition the water surrounding the outside of the keel will have a cooling effect. If possible it is best to use stainless steel to make the coils or condenser if one is to be made, stainless steel loses its heat far quicker than copper and will therefore also have a greater cooling effect than copper pipe. There is one problem

with the use of stainless steel, it is very difficult, if not impossible to solder, be it with soft or silver solder. Using special flux, joints can be made that appear sound but tests have proved that after a period of time they are quite likely to break down.

All that is needed of course to join piping to a fitting is a nipple that the union can force into the mating pipe. Stainless steel is very difficult material to solder, fortunately we don't need to, the ends of the pipe can be flared out and providing the shape is reasonably near to the receiving section, it will do the job nicely, particularly if an 'O' ring is inserted. Stainless steel varies considerably in quality, which means that some examples will be too hard to flare and ensure a good shape. The best type of piping to use is that used for fuel and clutch hydraulics in motorcars, which is sold in stores specialising in motorcar parts. It can also be obtained for next to nothing from car breakers' yards, but in that case will need to be cleaned thoroughly to get rid of every trace of the hydraulic fluid, before using it in a boat.

It is worth considering the use of multiple water tanks for storage, passing the water from one to the other, this will not only mean that more water can be carried, but it may also mean additional ballast for the boat. If more than one tank is used they should be arranged in such a way that water is sent to and taken away evenly from each. Water is quite heavy and a tank full on one side of a boat could put it on an uneven keel.

The condensed water is unlikely to become completely cold, using such a primitive form of condenser and this is all to the good as it will mean that with warm water going in, less heat will be needed to turn it back into steam.

Like so many things in a modelling hobby the best solution for a particular model will almost certainly be found by trial and error. The solution will vary not only from district to district but possibly also from model to model and it may well be that two models will behave quite differently when using the same water supply.

3
General Construction

It is possible to make an engine without the use of a lathe, but a means of drilling holes will be essential, apart from that construction can be purely by hand using basic tools such as hack saws and files, but in addition some marking out tools will be a necessity. These are rule, scriber, dividers and centre punch and unless the centre punch is of the automatic type a small hammer will be required to enable it to be used. It will also be necessary to have some means of heating the metal for soldering and as a soldering iron is unlikely to supply enough heat, this means a small blowlamp. The type that can be purchased in a DIY store will do and it should also be capable of supplying enough heat to make a small boiler. Whatever happens do not be tempted to get one of the small pencil type of torches, while these would be fine for soldering small pieces, they will not give enough heat for our purposes. Of course as soldering is to take place some solder and a suitable flux will also be needed. Providing tubing is used for the cylinder block the above tools are quite sufficient to make an oscillating engine or even a slide valve type. The most important thing by far is to take care with the marking out, on either type the position of the steam and exhaust ports is critical if the engine is to be a success.

Although an engine can be made with hand tools only, in order to make one from scratch, a lathe is desirable

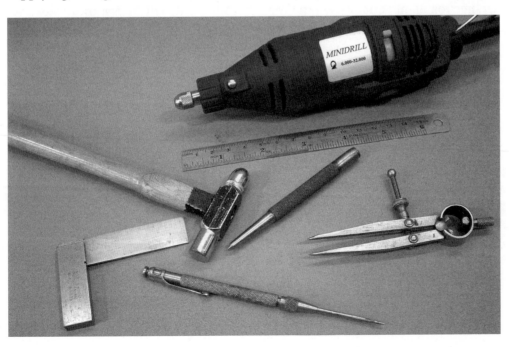

A selection of small hand tools that are sufficient to build a simple oscillating engine.

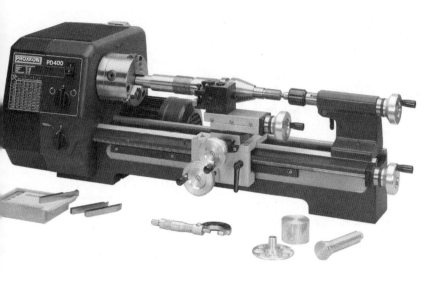

Another useful small lathe, the Proxon seen here with several useful accessories.

and there are a number of suitable small models on the market, such as the Unimat, Cowell, Proxon and Peatol, prices vary considerably according to the equipment that is bought with the lathe. All the above are truly portable and can easily be kept in a box indoors and used on an ordinary table. A number of slightly larger lathes are imported from the Far East and are available under a variety of names, they are generally made from the same or similar castings and so apart from the colour and name are all more or less the same, although some suppliers do arrange for slight variations in the way of equipment. Pre-owned small lathes are frequently available at almost knock down prices, either through a dealer or by private treaty.

It would be nice to cover in depth how to use the lathe and other equipment during the course of this book, sadly there is not sufficient room but the necessary information will be given about how to machine the various components when the construction of actual engines, etc. is dealt with. Even so for anyone who has never used machine tools before it is recommended that a book covering

the subject is purchased, a number are available at quite reasonable prices and one cannot have too much knowledge on the subject. It is also a good thing if a friend or relative who has an intimate knowledge of machining is asked for some help. However it is necessary to be very careful when doing this, there are fewer and fewer skilled machinists around these days and sometimes the person from whom help is requested does not themselves have a true understanding of machines. Help is given with the best intention but it is something like the 'blind leading the blind' and it is not unknown for wrong advice to have been given although done with the best of intentions.

Do not be tempted to buy a lathe that only has a three jaw self-centring chuck, it will be very limiting as it will only be possible to work on round or hexagon bar stock and nothing else. The only thing that can be done to that is to reduce it in diameter and perhaps drill it, adding either an internal or external thread if a suitable tap or die is available. If a four jaw independent chuck is available it will be far more flexible. That type of chuck has four jaws each of which moves independently and so allows rectangular bar stock and even certain casting to be fitted in it.

Setting a 4-jaw independent chuck

Many inexperienced metal workers do not like the four jaw independent chuck as they find it difficult to set up work accurately when using one, yet this need not be so. Start by opening the jaws so that there is clearance round the work to be set up and line up the axis point, (which if possible should be marked out and lightly centre punched). with the lathe tailstock centre. Move each jaw until the lathe tailstock centre lines up with the centre punch mark; the chuck will then grip the work very lightly. At that stage it should be near to being in the correct position, but will not be right.

If the work is to be machined across its end face the final lining up process can be done with the tailstock centre and should be covered with chalk ready for the process. If the end cannot be machined then put an ordinary lead pencil in the tailstock chuck; use a round pencil otherwise the point will not be true with the centre. Bring either the tailstock centre or the pencil to a point where it just touches the work and then rotate the lathe by hand. The centre or pencil will mark the work, the centre point having removed a circle of chalk and it will be possible to see how near to running true it is. If you have got it correct, forget about model boats and run out and buy a National Lottery ticket quickly as if you are that lucky you must win the jackpot.

Assuming the inevitable and the component is not running true, line up the position that is furthest from the centre or pencil, with yourself. Undo the jaw immediately behind that point, by about a quarter of a turn of the chuck key and tighten the one nearest to you by the same amount. Rotate the lathe by hand again and repeat the adjustment in exactly the same way and keep on doing it until the central point is running true. It will probably be necessary to re-chalk or rub out the pencil marks a few times and the amount of turn on the chuck key should be gradually reduced as the progress

goes on, but eventually it will be right. The important thing to remember is that only one operation is used that is the gradual tightening of the nearest jaw after very slightly releasing the one furthest away. It does not take long to learn the technique, but the temptation to think that a better adjustment can be obtained by adjusting the other jaws will only lead to frustration. When it comes down to it, different jaws are being adjusted each time, as they will vary depending on the movement of the work.

To true up a piece of square or rectangular bar, the same technique

A useful combined milling machine and lathe the Unimat 5 can manage every aspect of building model marine engines.

A four jaw is a very versatile means of work holding and is shown here being used to drill the bores of a cylinder block, something that could not be done with the three jaw.

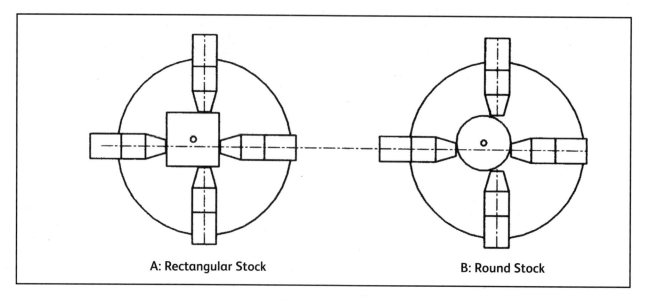

A: Rectangular Stock

B: Round Stock

A. For square or rectangular stock, adjust on horizontal jaws only no matter what no. jaw that is.

B. to set round stock, the vertical jaws must be released before adjustment.

can be used, except that instead of lining up to a datum mark, tighten the jaws sufficiently to provide a safe grip, then start the lathe and just bring the cutting tool to give the tiniest shave to the metal. Stop the lathe and have a look, it is possible to see which one or perhaps two edges have received the attention of the tool. We can now loosen the jaw directly behind while tightening the one nearest to us. And so on until the amount taken off each of the four edges are exactly the same, again do not be tempted to adjust any other jaw except the two directly in line. This is a remarkably accurate method of centring the bar stock, as it is surprisingly easy to judge the amount of metal that has been removed, without recourse to any measuring aid.

Round bar adjustment can be a little more difficult as one has to take into account the curve of the diameter and this can mean that it will not be possible initially to adjust in the same way. If the jaw has gone to a point where the radius is still rising behind it then a second jaw will have to be opened in order to move the work back. Once some sort of alignment has been achieved the procedure can be the same as before.

When the bar is near to being lined up the same idea of just shaving off a minute piece can be followed and in this case also it is easy to see when the bar is running true.

Whatever the work is that is being set up, before machining all four jaws must be tightened by an even amount, i.e. a tenth or an eighth of a turn or something similar. The final tightening should be via opposite jaws i.e. one and three then two and four or vice versa.

The methods referred to above can give a reasonable degree of accuracy, but for absolute accuracy it will be necessary to use some form of mechanical aid and an experienced machinist will use a centre finder and clock gauge for the purpose. Nevertheless the method of jaw adjustment remains the same as detailed above. Once again readers proposing to use a lathe who have no experience of doing so are advised to obtain a good book on the subject and to read it thoroughly and to have a little practice before attempting to make an engine.

Smoothing port faces

A task that will have to be tackled when making either oscillating or slide valve engines is to get the port faces smooth and true, in the case of the slide valve the valve face also needs to be smooth and accurate. The more accurate these are the better the engine will work and time spent polishing them will amply repay itself in the efficiency of the engine.

Again there is no black magic about the process, the port face, port block or valve is placed on a piece of fine abrasive paper that is laid on a true flat surface. The latter may be the stumbling block as finding a surface that is absolutely true may not be that simple. The professional will use a surface plate, but not too many of those are found in the workshops of amateurs. Thick plate glass is often quoted as a good alternative, but getting a piece of ½ ins. thick glass is not as easy as it might seem. Most glaziers deal in nothing more than quarter plate and that cannot always be guaranteed to be flat.

Frequently thick chipboard will do, it is made to quite a high standard and by checking with a straight edge it will be possible to find out if a piece is accurate or not. Another good alternative for anyone using one of the larger lathes with a flat bed, such as a Myford is to use the bed of that, it is a bit limited in width but as long as the component being worked on is not too large it should be adequate.

When the flat surface has been established lay the part to be dealt with on the abrasive paper and rotate it in a figure of eight movement until the whole of the face takes on a dull appearance, it is then ready for use. It may be necessary to use several grades of paper in order to get it right, each grade being finer than the last. Do not be tempted to use anything other than the figure of eight

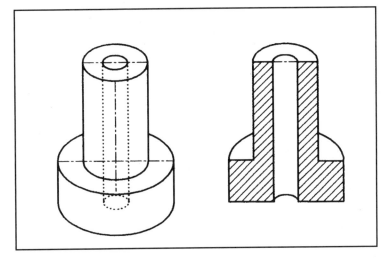

movement, rubbing it up and down can lead to a rocking movement that will mean the edges are lower than the centre and yet the whole surface may have taken on the flat appearance that is wanted. A circular movement will often put pressure on one side and that too will mean an uneven surface.

For a really first class surface a substance called Engineers' Blue can be used, it is a rather messy substance that is rubbed on the surface to be worked on. When that surface is rubbed over the abrasive any area that has been missed will remain blue and honing can continue until the colour has completely disappeared.

Soldering

As with lathe work, soldering is something of a black art to the uninitiated, full instructions on how to go about things will be given during the course of this book and so there should be no need to worry. The most important thing to be remembered about soldering is that both surfaces must be thoroughly cleaned before starting and once heat is applied they will rapidly oxidise, flux prevents oxidisation as long as the work is not overheated so ensure the area

Simple guide bush to keep a tap square to a surface whilst cutting a thread.

27

to be soldered has received a liberal coating of flux, before applying heat. It is also essential to remember that the solder must always be melted by the heat of the metal and not the heat of the flame or soldering iron, only if the heat of the material melts it, will the result be a sound joint.

Threading

Taps are used for internal threading and dies for work that is done externally and both processes are reasonably easy. The threads that will be used are quite small and care is needed in making them. In the case of taps it is very easy if they do not go squarely into the hole to break them, and if the same thing happens with a die then there is every chance of the work snapping inside the die. It is essential therefore to ensure that both taps and dies fit squarely over the work, lathe owners can make simple tapping guides that will ensure correct alignment. Guides for dies are not quite such an easy matter and if possible it is best to thread items while they are held in the lathe. The die holder, if an ordinary hand held one, can be guided by the tailstock; better still use a proper tailstock die holder if one is available. Tapping can also be carried out with the work in the lathe but the lathe should be carefully rotated by hand to do so.

The rotation of both taps and dies should be reversed after a turn or two otherwise swarf will build up and cause them to jam, which is another cause of breakage. If the thread is long then the tap or die should be completely removed from time to time and the recesses cleared of swarf and dirt. Not only is a dirty tap or die prone to breakage but the dirt can also completely ruin a thread. The use of a tapping and threading compound is advisable, except when working on copper that will subsequently be silver soldered, in that instance it is just a case of withdrawing the tap more frequently. Using any sort of cutting compound on copper is likely to interfere with the work of the flux when the metal is heated.

Measurements

This book is not a construction manual, although there are a number of constructional articles, it is mainly intended to give advice to those wishing to build models and it is for those readers to make their own decisions on the models they might wish to make. Because of the origin of the material contained herein most measurements are in imperial format; likewise most of the threads are quoted as British Association or BA. A suitable chart will allow for easy thread conversion but in doing so attention should be given to the pitch of the thread as well as the diameter. In addition it is rarely practical to convert imperial to metric measurements, a straight mathematical conversion can give figures with decimal places that are difficult to work to. Anyone wishing to convert the measurements in any of the drawings is therefore advised to make a new drawing rounding the figures to the nearest half millimetre and in doing so ensuring that the various parts will match with each other. It is always advisable to work by fitting parts together, rather than to make two components to measurements and then hope they will fit each other.

The above is a very brief resume of the techniques required for making model steam plants, it would take a whole volume to describe everything in detail and so further information on the subject, if required, must be the subject of personal research.

4

Oscillating Engines

Because of its sheer simplicity the oscillating engine is very popular with marine modellers. There are a considerable number of models of various types available commercially, either for home construction or as finished models. Quite a large number are purchased and they are relatively cheap to buy but sadly not all those that are sold are well designed and therefore do not give the performance that they should. Several model engineering suppliers, market sets of parts for home construction, these vary from basic castings, where one obtains all other parts to complete the engine for oneself, to complete kits, down to the last nut and bolt. It will depend on the facilities available to the individual as well as their knowledge of metalworking as to which road to take.

Oscillating engines tend to be considered as lacking in power and difficult to start as well as having a tendency to leak steam all over the place. None of these are true if the engine is designed and built properly. After all, the oscillating engine was used in full sized practice for many years, particularly for marine work.

Let us start by taking a brief look at how an oscillating engine actually works. No doubt all readers will know that steam has to enter a closed cylinder in such a way that it will push a close

A little Vee format oscillating engine powers this very attractive steam launch of John Thompson.

fitting piston along the length of that cylinder. It is here that the simplicity of the oscillating engine comes into its own, the steam is allowed in by simply lining up two holes. One of these is in the cylinder or an area of it known as the port face, while the other is in the port block. The port block is only a name given to the component, which as a general rule will also form the frame of the engine. The piston is joined by a rod to a crank that converts the linear motion to rotary. In order to give the piston enough momentum to return to whence it came, so that it can receive another dollop of steam, a flywheel is used, the momentum of that keeping things moving.

Of course the steam that pushed the piston along the cylinder now has to escape and steam being what it is, there is about twice as much of it as there was in the first place, as it has expanded. If we just have our two original holes lined up, more steam is continuously entering the cylinder and the spent steam cannot get out, because that coming in is at a higher pressure than that going out and we have a complete impasse.

Like all good stories there should be a happy ending and the only way to get that is to allow that spent steam to escape. The people who worked things out in the first place thought that one out as well achieved it by making another hole for the steam to exit. It is of course essential that the original hole in the cylinder that accepted the steam in the first place be lined up with the new one that will allow the steam to exhaust.

This is done in the easiest possible way by simply fitting a pivot to the cylinder so that it can swing from the position where it was when it accepted the steam, to the other side where it can escape from the other hole. In doing so it blocks off the original hole in the port block, preventing any fresh steam from entering. In this the simplest oscillator, the piston is only pushed in one direction and it is said to be a single acting engine. More complex types arrange for the piston to be pushed in both directions are described as double acting. That is basically all there is to an oscillating engine, the pivot on which the cylinder swings backwards and forwards, or put another way, oscillates, a hole to let the steam in and one to let it out. What could possibly be easier?

One of the secrets in making a reliable and efficient engine is to get the relationship between that pivot and the two holes, or ports as they are known, exactly right and that is something we will come to shortly.

Firstly let us take brief look at a problem that is general to any single cylinder engine which is that it will usually only start if given some assistance; this is a result of the engine stopping at a position where the inlet valve is fully closed.

It is usual to rotate the flywheel by hand in order to get the engine started, which is all very well when standing on the bank but rather difficult if the boat is in the middle of a lake, particularly if the water is very deep. This is an area where a single cylinder oscillating engine has an advantage over other types of single cylinder engines as the problem can be overcome by fitting a light spring between the crank and a fixed point on the engine frame, so that when steam is cut off the spring pulls the cylinder across to the position where the steam port is open. It is an idea that works very well but the spring must be very light, otherwise it will absorb all the power of the engine.

In an attempt to offset starting problems without the aid of a spring some people opt to use a higher boiler pressure, this does not solve anything, if the cylinder and engine ports are not in line no matter what the pressure is raised to, the steam cannot enter the cylinder the engine is not going to work.

A very large proportion of commercially marketed engines are constructed in such a way that they will only rotate at a very fast speed, something, which is not desirable in a boat; and is frequently solved by fitting gearing to make the propeller run at a more suitable speed. The gearing inevitably absorbs some of the power of the engine, which could even mean that a boat requires a larger engine to cope with the loss, which in turn can result in an out of scale appearance. In fact all that the gears are doing is making up for what amounts to a bad design in the first place.

One of or perhaps the only reason for this, particularly with engines that are commercially made is that they are built with a wide spacing between the two ports; this is usually done for convenience. It may mean that the designer has sought to decrease the height of the engine by increasing the gap between the ports. This is where building the engine at home can be advantageous as it will be possible to bring the two closer together, ensuring that most of the problems immediately disappear, so let us have a look to see how this can be done. Looking at the layout as a whole we can see that the ports are positioned in direct relationship to the pivot and crank, and if the relationship can be set in such a way that the ports are closer together, the engine will run slowly as well as start easier. The ideal distance between the ports is just a tiny bit more than one diameter of the port itself. This ensures that as soon as the crank causes the cylinder to tip, the steam inside can escape and as soon as it has escaped, the other port is opening for more steam.

Designing an engine

Not only are oscillating engines very simple things to make, they are also very straightforward to design and it is very easy to draw up ones own oscillating engine on paper, using nothing more than a rule and compass. In so doing one can eliminate or at the very least decrease the problems associated with layout. On a piece of paper, draw a straight line to represent the centre line of the engine and mark off the proposed height that the engine is intended to be. At a suitable point from the base, use the compasses to draw a circle that represents the crank throw. The stroke of the cylinder will be twice that of the throw of the crank. Draw a line across the centre line and at right angles to it, so that it passes exactly through the position where the compass point intersected the line. Where that line meets the circle is the position of the crank at 90 deg.

Mark the proposed position of the cylinder pivot on the centre line and then the position at which the ports are intended to be. Draw a line between

the 90 deg. point of the crank circle, through the pivot point and just above the position of the ports, then mark from the port position at 90 degs. and where it crossed the line will be an approximate position for the port. It will not be quite right but it will give one a rough idea to work to. If the port position is too wide, then move towards the centre line until the required width is found, draw a line from there through the pivot to the horizontal line of the crank, where it intersects will be the position of the crank pin. It may be necessary to extend or decrease the distance between the crankshaft and pivot pin in order to obtain a suitable crank throw as also it determines the length of the stroke of the piston. If a suitable compromise between stroke and width between ports can be found that is fine and all that remains is to improve the accuracy by setting the compass on the pivot point and drawing an arc through the centre of the ports. Because the engine oscillates they will be on an arc instead of a straight line so now readjust the setting out line so that it goes through the port centres as placed on the arc, this will also involve

In this steam plant, the builder has cleverly disguised it's over-size appearance. The boiler specified for the boat has cross tubes and on this boat is fitted particularly neatly.

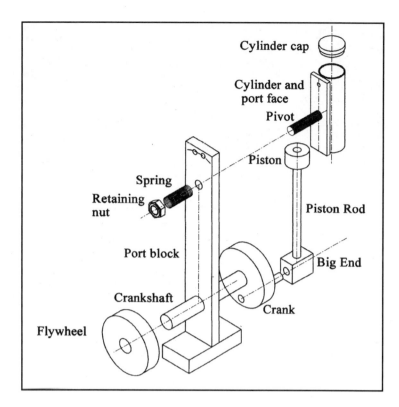

Layout of a simple, single cylinder oscillating engine. More advanced designs are simply a case of development of this layout.

a slight alteration to the crank throw.

The above gives one an exact setting out for the engine layout and except on a very large engine, the difference between the ports set on an arc and those on the straight line is minuscule. For the sake of convenience when designing an engine many builders prefer to use the straight line as it is a great deal easier than trying to use an arc We will see later how to correct this small error when building anyway and so it will be up to the individual as to which method they wish to use to mark the engine out.

An engine built with an average model boat in mind, using the above methods of design will work, but it will almost definitely suffer, either from a stroke that is too short, or from ports that are so wide apart that the engine needs to rotate at a high speed in order to run smoothly. Assuming the stroke has been set correctly then the crank must remain the same length and the port positions altered. Therefore we

must bring them closer together, draw the line again through the pivot until it reaches the width of the crank, it will be found that the engine layout has lengthened considerably and in all probability will now be out of proportion with the boat. So yet another solution is needed.

Slightly countersink the ports, either the two on the port block, or the one on the cylinder face, it doesn't matter which, this has the effect of reducing the unwanted dead spot. In fact there is no reason why all three should not be slightly countersunk if it is necessary to do so to get more efficient operation. The idea works well enough, but one has to be a little careful to avoid the port on the cylinder moving outside the width of the port block and thus becoming open to the atmosphere. If a countersink is to be used therefore it will be prudent to check that the width of the port block is sufficient to prevent this from happening.

What is really needed is for the ports to be set closer to the pivot, there will then by no reason why they cannot be the preferred distance apart and the stroke as long as one wishes. So it is back to the drawing board and redesign the engine with the ports much closer to the pivot, so that as the cylinder oscillates they all line up nicely. We cannot of course drill through the cylinder port to allow the steam in, when it will be entering about half way up, so a hole is drilled down vertically and the port that enters the cylinder drilled in the correct place. Both the outside of that and the hole drilled lengthways, which is known as a transfer port are sealed off by tapping them and fitting a short length of brass screw. The position now is that although the steam and exhaust are moved from steam block to cylinder somewhere near the pivot point, but the steam will enter and exhaust at the end of the piston stroke and we have a very efficient engine as the result.

The 3 sketches below illustrate this, showing in the first one a typical layout with a 1in stroke and ¾in between ports and pivot. In order to get an engine of reasonable proportions 2in has been allowed between pivot and crankshaft centres. This works out to 3/8in between port centres, the ports being shown as 1/8in diameter which is considerably in excess of the diameter required for this size of engine.

The second sketch shows the effect of increasing the distance between pivot and crankshaft centres to 2-9/16in and the port centres are now considerable closer, although as shown the distance would be too great for correct diameter ports. While this layout would improve running qualities of the engine it has also increased its height to the point where for many boats it would be out

of proportion. If we had taken the ports closer together and kept the distance between pivot and crank centres as it was, the effect would have been to reduce the stroke of the engine, resulting in a loss of power.

The third sketch shows the effect of drilling the ports closer to the pivot and then transferring them to the correct position between cylinder and port block. This has reduced the height of the engine, but allowed the crank throw

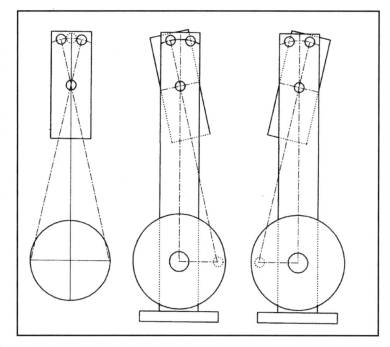

This drawing illustrates the priciple of the oscillating engine. The central port in the cylinder block can be seen to alternatively line-up with the steam admission and exhaust port as the Flywheel rotates and the cylinder oscillates from side to side.

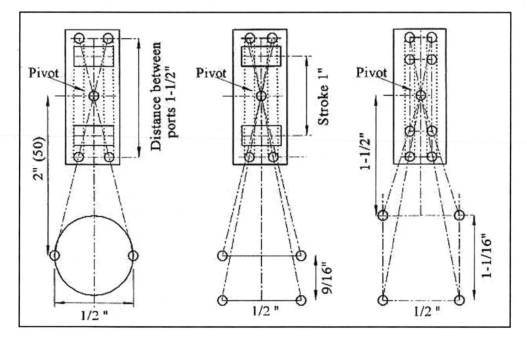

The shape and size of the engine is is dictated by the distance between the cylinder pivot and the crank.

to remain the same. To make the transfer it is simply a case of drilling between the ports at the top and then plugging the outer end of the hole with a screw, unless of course the hole drilled is to be opened out for inlet and exhaust purposes.

The above will certainly improve the efficiency of the engine, but there is still more that we can do, in particular we can reduce friction. Forget the more centralised ports for a while and return to the original concept of an oscillating engine. We have the cylinder port face, rubbing over the port block as the engine oscillates and the friction is causing some loss of power. If two grooves are made between the port area and pivot that friction is considerably reduced, giving greater efficiency and in addition as a rule it results in better mating surfaces as well.

When it comes to the engine with the centralised ports it is a case of machining away the area immediately outside the ports leaving the rest free then the only part creating any friction is that immediately around the port area. This is also of course the area round the pivot, so two potential causes of friction have immediately been removed. This method of placing the ports close to the pivot is the one that was used in full sized practice when oscillating engines were in regular use.

This area where the two sets of ports mate is a potential source of steam leakage and needs to be very well fitted. As well as being smoothed on a piece of abrasive paper The two surfaces should be lapped together, by moving the cylinder backwards and forwards on the port block until the surface of the two is absolutely flat. The finest possible grinding paste is needed for the purpose and either metal polish or toothpaste, both of which do a very fine job, are ideal. It is not a quick operation and the more time spent lapping the two parts together the more efficient the engine will be. There is a substance that can be used for grinding the parts together that is more efficient than either of the above, it is called diamantine and is favoured by clock makers for polishing clock wheels, etc. It may be difficult to obtain but would be well worth the effort involved in finding some.

After lapping the two parts together they should be thoroughly washed in white spirit, using a soft brush to clean the ports out, there should be no trace of grinding paste remaining under any circumstances.

In the early days of steam, when oscillating engines were in common use, the movement of the cylinders was considered as a possible danger during rough weather. On large vessels the engine or engines were turned upside down and the cylinders placed at the bottom, thus keeping weight as low as possible. The idea was successful enough for it to be continued after non-oscillating engines became the normal source of power. Gradually fixed cylinder engines had the cylinders moved to a higher position, possibly mainly for ease of maintenance, but even then large oscillating engines continued to have them at the bottom. Most model boats are of course fitted with engines with the cylinders at the top, but the design by Henry Greenly, that was produced in 1944 and is illustrated on Page 134 and 135, follows the true pattern of an oscillating engine.

Double acting engines.

Up to now the suggested design has been for the engine to be single acting, with steam and exhaust entering and exiting at one end of the cylinder, this is the easiest type of engine to make and made in this fashion engines will work very satisfactorily. In some ways though this is a wasteful way of working as the engine is only developing half the power it is capable of. The cylinders can easily be made double acting, with steam entering either side of the piston, thus doubling the power. Most work on this principle and whilst the single acting engine, is very easy to build the extra effort to make it double acting is well worthwhile. A single acting engine can be made using only hand tools, but a small lathe will be needed to make a double acting one.

It is simply a case of mirroring the port arrangement at the other end of the cylinder, that end will have to be sealed of course so that the steam can be contained, in such a way that the piston rod can pass through. This is done with a gland arrangement and on models it is usual to make the gland in the form of a simple screw on nut. For authenticity it should really be held in place with studs and nuts and if anyone is looking to make an open boat with an authentic looking engine, that is the way it should be done. With a single acting engine the cylinder cover can be soldered in place as there will never be a need to remove it, indeed the cylinder could even be made from solid, with a blind bore. Although not the most desirable method, there is no reason why the bottom cover on a double acting engine cannot also be soldered in place, and if tubing has been used to make the cylinder it is almost certain that it will be the only way of fixing it. To do this it is essential that the piston is located at exactly the right position in the bore, so that it is just clear of the ports at each end of the stroke; this has to be attended to before the bottom cover can be soldered in place.

It is much better to secure the bottom cover with screws so that it is possible to pull the piston out of the cylinder when there is any maintenance needed. This will mean that unless a particularly thick walled tube happens to be available, which is not generally the case, the cylinder has to be made of solid material, leaving sufficient area round the edges to make the holes for the screws.

Whether to make the engine single or double acting is a matter of personal choice that may well be governed by the size of boat the engine is to be used in. A single acting engine can be made much more compact than a double acting one and therefore might be the right choice, a certain amount of additional power can be obtained by making a small increase in the diameter of the cylinders, which will offset the fact that the engine is only single acting.

A common design fault is to make the ports too large. There is no need for large ports, which in fact just waste steam and so reduce the length of time the boiler can feed the engine. If the ports are oversize the steam does not get the opportunity to expand as it should and less power will be generated than would be the case with smaller ports. For cylinders with bores of ¼in (6mm) ports of a diameter of 1/64in or 0.5mm diameter are usually quite sufficient. For cylinders 5/16in (8mm) up to 3/8in (10mm) diameter 1/32in or 1mm will do, other sizes are pro rata.

Multiple cylinders

So far we have only dealt with single cylinder engines. We do see quite a few boats that are powered by them and there are a number of finished models and simple boat kits made for that type of engine. Generally they are marketed with the younger enthusiast in mind and there is no doubt that they are an ideal introduction to model steam boating. It is also recognised that the less experienced model maker with limited equipment might not wish to make anything more complicated.

For those with only slightly more equipment and just a tiny bit more expertise, making a twin cylinder engine is not all that difficult. A multi-cylindered engine will be more efficient than a single cylindered one and should in theory at least run in a smoother fashion. It is therefore advisable to fit an engine with at least two cylinders whenever possible and there are several configurations that can be used. Various designs have been published in model magazines from time to time. An engine that has quite an authentic appearance can be designed even though it is an oscillating engine. Most models will have the cylinders in line with each other, but it must be remembered that some open boats have them in the 'V' configuration and there is no reason why that should not be used on a model. It is possible to use a large number or permutations of cylinder arrangements in order to make a suitable engine.

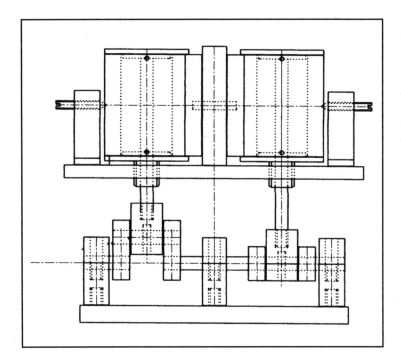

A popular in-line twin cylinder oscillating engine. The cylinders are fabricated from tube and strip. The design can be adapted to any size and is thus very useful.

Method of fabricating a cylinder from tube and flat material

Construction

Different people will have various ideas on where to start construction and ultimately the choice must be an individual one, however for the sake of this book the cylinder or cylinders are the suggested starting point. Commercial tubing can be used successfully for making cylinders but more often than not has a very big drawback, it will usually be found that the bore is far from smooth. This means that the piston is going to pass through in a series of steps, each of which means a potential loss of steam or a tight spot

and so it will be necessary to smooth them out. There are a variety of ways in which this can be done, the tube can be put in the lathe and a small boring tool run through it, the cuts must be very light and to do this it is best if the lathe is running at a high speed. Do not try and pass a drill through the tube with the lathe running as it will almost certainly bind up while you are doing so, the same applies to a reamer. A reamer can be used successfully and to do so the work should be mounted in the chuck with the reamer in the tailstock in the normal way and the lathe rotated by hand, so that any binding action can immediately be felt. White spirit or turpentine substitute should be used as a cutting lubricant. If, as is almost certain the tubing is to be subsequently soldered to another piece of metal, care must be taken to completely remove all traces of the liquid as it will prevent the solder from adhering.

Not everyone will possess a boring bar small enough to go through the tube in which case it can be lapped. Take a length of wooden dowel about 4mm or 5/32in smaller than the bore of the tube, put a saw cut in one end and lay two small pieces of emery cloth in the slot, back to back. The tube can be held in the vice, while the lap that has just been made can be rotated slowly and moved in and out, do not let it come right out. The ideal tool with which to rotate the lap is a battery operated DIY hand drill with an electronic speed control using the lowest possible speed It does not take all that long and it is possible to get a really smooth bore in this fashion. Care must be taken not to allow the lap to come out of the ends, as doing so will cause bell mouthing.

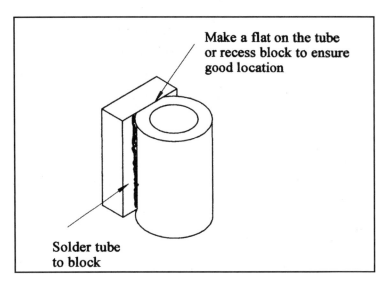

Make a flat on the tube or recess block to ensure good location

Solder tube to block

Using bar stock

Far greater accuracy can be obtained if bar material is used and it need not necessarily be round, although that is how we tend to think of cylinders. It is as well to remember that on oscillating engines and also on a slide valve engine, at least the face of the cylinder where the ports are situated must be flat. Therefore starting with square material makes a great deal of sense as that flat face is already there. In full size practice many cylinders, particularly in the case of multi-cylindered engines were not round at all and were nearer to a square shape. Hexagon bar is also worth considering as again it gives us a face that is already flat ready for the ports to be drilled.

The obvious advantage of bar stock over the use of tubing is that it is possible to obtain a really smooth bore. It is also possible to leave a thicker outer wall so that cylinder covers can be screwed in place rather than soldered as will be the case if tubing is used. Things should not be taken too far in this direction as if the cylinder wall is too thick it will absorb heat and make the engine less efficient, an effect that can be reduced in some respects by thinning the walls in between the ends and centre portion, leaving sufficient material for fixing the cylinder covers and pivot.

The Port Face

Whether tube or solid material has been used, the next operation if it is round is the same and involves soldering a piece of flat brass or bronze strip to the cylinder. After thoroughly deburring the strip make a very shallow saw cut centrally along its length and then with a round file convert the cut into a round

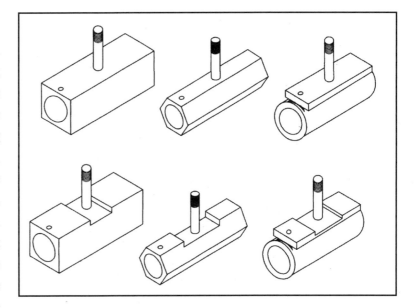

Many different forms of bar stock can be used to make cylinders. The lower 3 drawings show the port face recessed to improve efficiency.

groove. Take every precaution to keep the width and depth of the groove the same throughout its length. Owners of lathes that have a vertical slide can put the strip on that and mill the groove, which will be far more accurate than filing; a ball nosed cutter should be used if available. If the facilities of a milling machine or a milling attachment are available then that of course can be used in preference to the vertical slide.

The port face and cylinder have to be joined and this can be done with soft solder. Some may feel that silver soldering would be better and there is no doubt that a stronger job would be the result. However it is doubtful if the groove in the block and the radius of the cylinder will tally exactly and any discrepancy will need to be taken up with solder. This is not as easy to do with silver solder particularly for the less experienced and should therefore only be attempted by somebody with experience.

The port face should be laid on a flat heatproof surface, like a brick and flux applied liberally along the groove. The cylinder is then put on top and should protrude a tiny bit beyond the end. Take

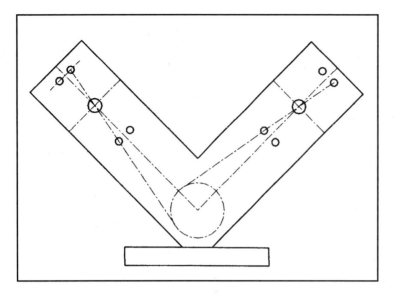

With a simple alteration to the frame, a "V" formation results. If too small an angle is used, the big-ends will bind. This can be cured by a split big-end arrangement. Slide or piston valve engines can be built using the same principle.

plenty of time to make sure the cylinder and port face are lined up correctly and only when certain of this, should the work be heated and solder applied. If the cylinder cap is to be soldered in place, then it should be done at the same time as the joining of cylinder and port face. The use of square or hexagon bar to make the cylinder will generally mean that there is no need of a separate port face as the ports and pivot can be put in one of the flats.

Although the pivot pin can be soldered in place it is best to thread a short section of it and to tap the hole in the cylinder assembly. The pin should be made of stainless steel but there is no harm in the adjusting nut being brass or steel. Some builders like to make a knurled nut for this position because it is easier to adjust without having to resort to the use of a spanner

The port block

The port block is also referred to as the steam block and it contains the ports, pivot bearing and the crank bearing. Whether the latter is a separate bearing or just a hole through the port block will depend on the thickness of the block. If it is ¼ in or 6mm thick

then it is probably suitable to act as the bearing, if anything less than that it would be advisable to make a separate bearing and secure it to the port block with retaining compound. Although the steam ports can be drilled right through and connection made at the rear, this is not always convenient. It will therefore be necessary to transfer the position to another place, this can be done by drilling through the block and if necessary plugging the end of the hole.

Although marking out the ports has been dealt with that was only with reference to designing an engine. It is not wise to mark off the ports and drill them, as the chances of getting the required accuracy are pretty slim. A simple jig should be made that contains three or four holes. One to clear the crank pin, above that one to clear the pivot and also two holes for the steam ports; these are drilled on the centre line at the required distance above and below the pivot, depending on whether the engine is single or double acting. To use the jig slip it on the pivot with the lower hole over the crank pin and then set the crank to 90deg, the holes for the ports are then at the exact position on the necessary arc for the ports to be drilled. Put the crank to the other 90deg. position and do the same to get the pair or pairs of ports that are needed.

Perhaps some readers will feel that there has been a little too much emphasis on the oscillating engine, but it is by far the most popular home built type and is also the ideal introduction to making model engines. The techniques used will be in many ways similar to those required for a more complicated design and there is nothing like starting at the beginning.

Twin Cylinder In-line Oscillator

A compact double-acting marine engine utilising cylinders machined from square bar to incorporate the port faces. Appearance is improved by the use of round cylinder covers for this shorter than usual design

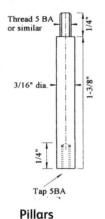

Pillars
6 off mild steel

Crankshaft Bearing
2 off brass

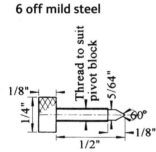

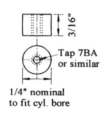

Outer Pivots
2 off mild steel
Fit lock-nuts

Piston
2 off stainless steel

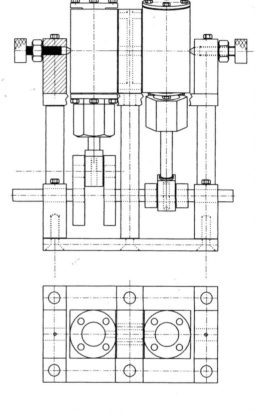

General Arrangement

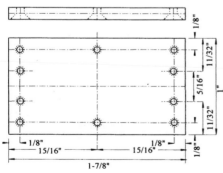

Engine Base
1 off 1/8in mild steel
All holes drilled 5BA clearance and countersunk

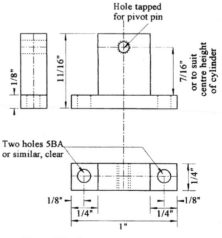

Pivot Blocks
2 off brass

NOT TO SCALE

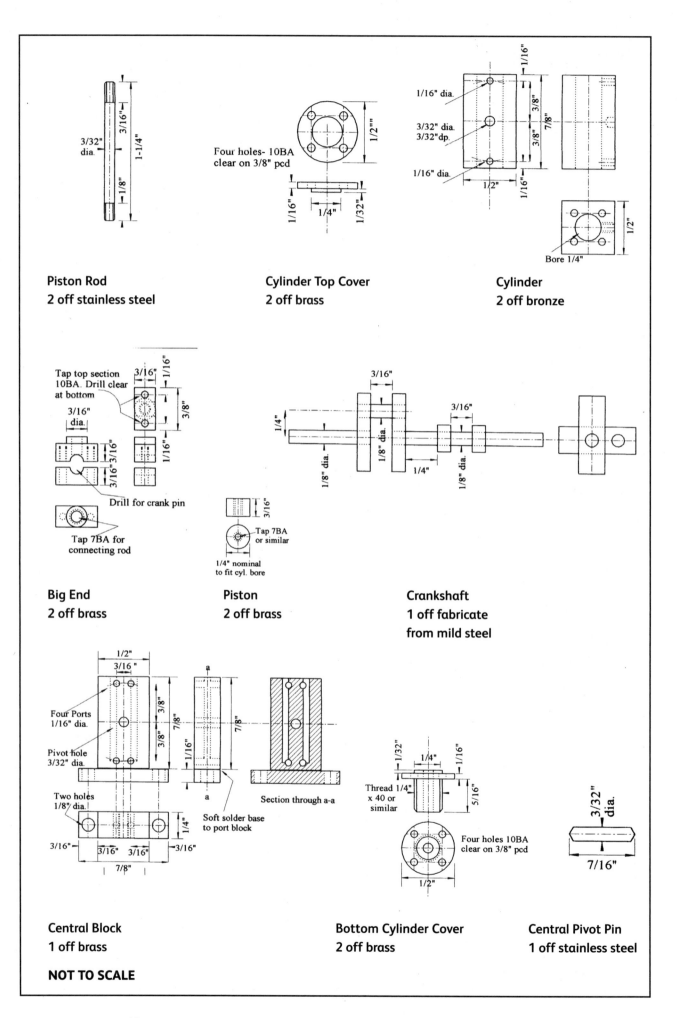

Piston Rod
2 off stainless steel

Cylinder Top Cover
2 off brass

Cylinder
2 off bronze

Big End
2 off brass

Piston
2 off brass

Crankshaft
1 off fabricate
from mild steel

Central Block
1 off brass

NOT TO SCALE

Bottom Cylinder Cover
2 off brass

Central Pivot Pin
1 off stainless steel

40

Twin Cylinder Horizontally Opposed Oscillator

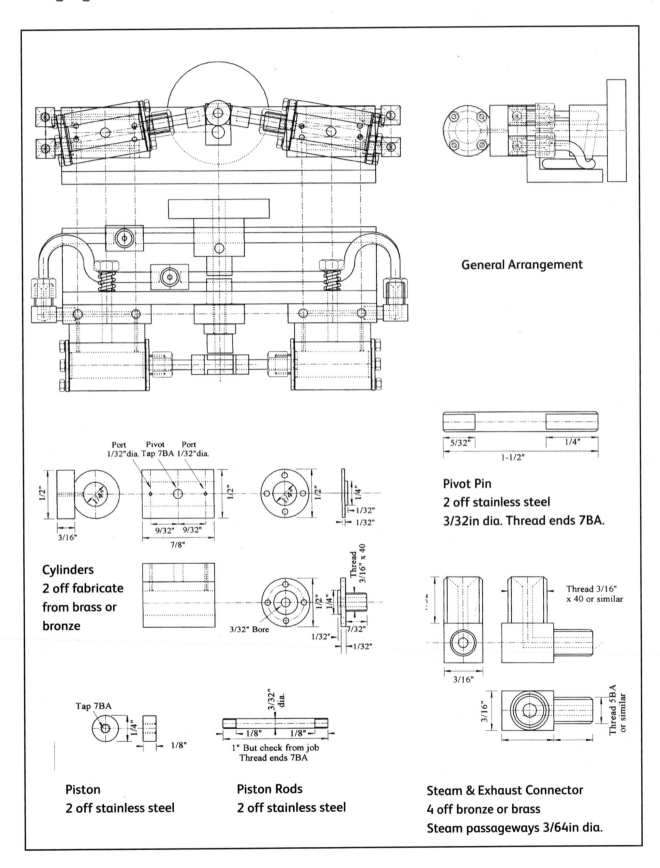

General Arrangement

Pivot Pin
2 off stainless steel
3/32in dia. Thread ends 7BA.

Cylinders
2 off fabricate
from brass or
bronze

Piston
2 off stainless steel

Piston Rods
2 off stainless steel

Steam & Exhaust Connector
4 off bronze or brass
Steam passageways 3/64in dia.

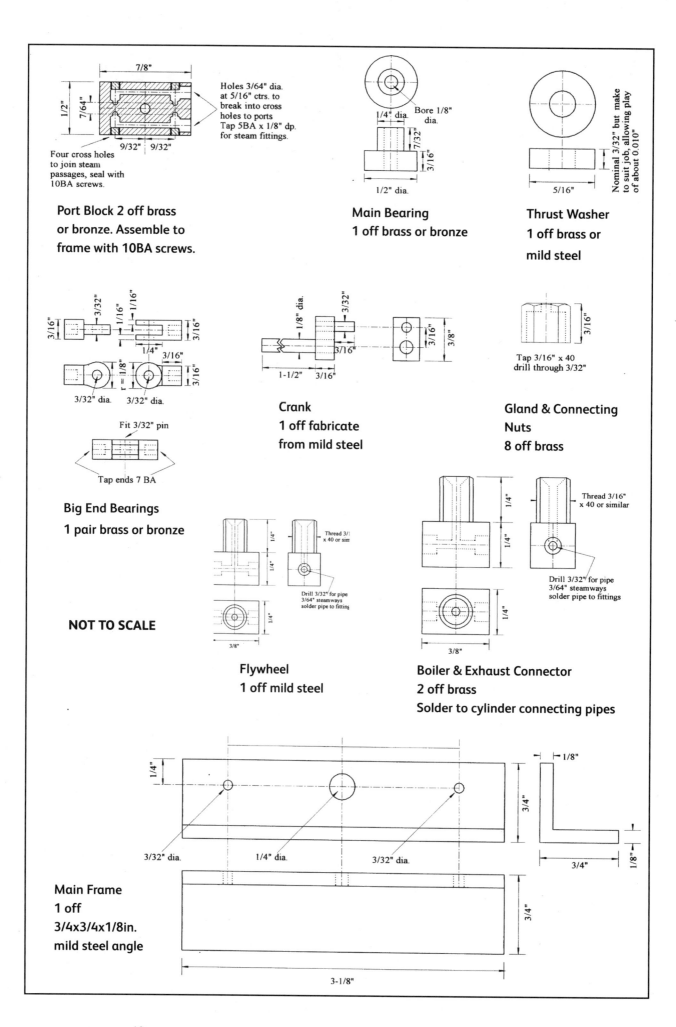

7/8"

1/2"

7/64"

9/32" 9/32"

Holes 3/64" dia.
at 5/16" ctrs. to
break into cross
holes to ports
Tap 5BA x 1/8" dp.
for steam fittings.

Four cross holes
to join steam
passages, seal with
10BA screws.

**Port Block 2 off brass
or bronze. Assemble to
frame with 10BA screws.**

Bore 1/8"
dia.

1/4" dia.

7/32"

3/16"

1/2" dia.

**Main Bearing
1 off brass or bronze**

Nominal 3/32" but make
to suit job, allowing play
of about 0.010"

3/16"

5/16"

**Thrust Washer
1 off brass or
mild steel**

3/32"

1/16"

1/16"

3/16"

1/16"

3/16"

1/4"

3/16"

3/16"

3/16"

r = 1/8"

3/32" dia.   3/32" dia.

Fit 3/32" pin

Tap ends 7 BA

**Big End Bearings
1 pair brass or bronze**

NOT TO SCALE

1/8" dia.

3/32"

3/16"

3/16"

3/8"

1-1/2"   3/16"

3/16"

**Crank
1 off fabricate
from mild steel**

3/16"

Tap 3/16" x 40
drill through 3/32"

**Gland & Connecting
Nuts
8 off brass**

1/4"

1/4"

1/4"

Thread 3/
x 40 or sim

Drill 3/32" for pipe
3/64" steamways
solder pipe to fitting

3/8"

**Flywheel
1 off mild steel**

1/4"

1/4"

1/4"

Thread 3/16"
x 40 or similar

Drill 3/32" for pipe
3/64" steamways
solder pipe to fittings

3/8"

**Boiler & Exhaust Connector
2 off brass
Solder to cylinder connecting pipes**

1/4"

3/92" dia.   1/4" dia.   3/32" dia.

1/8"

3/4"

3/4"

1/8"

3/4"

3-1/8"

**Main Frame
1 off
3/4x3/4x1/8in.
mild steel angle**

42

5

Slide Valve Engines

Following close on the heels of the oscillating engine as far as popularity is concerned is the slide valve and they are quite rightly a firm favourite amongst model makers. They are comparatively easy to make, are very reliable and as has been proved it is quite possible to make them to scale or near scale size for a boat. In addition the slide valve has a couple of advantages, there is no relationship between, crank, pivot and ports to worry about, so it is easier to design an engine to the size that one requires. Like the oscillating engine it is possible to make almost any configuration of cylinders and unlike the oscillator it is also possible to make them as compound or triple expansion models. It is not a great deal more difficult to design a slide valve engine than an oscillating one, but there are more parts and exactly how many will depend on the type of valve gear that one wishes to use. Once the few skills required to make model steam engines has been grasped it is possible to experiment for hours, using ones own ideas to perfect a personal design.

For those that have little or no knowledge of a steam engine let us start by explaining how a slide vale engine works. As with any steam engine a cylinder is needed together with end covers, a piston and piston rod. Some means of supporting the cylinder in the

form of a frame is also required. The cylinder can be in any position, vertical horizontal or at an angle, it will still work, whichever way round it is. The cylinder has a port face in the same way that the oscillating engine does, but the similarity ends there, because instead of having a pivot and two holes for the ports, the slide valve engine works in an entirely different way.

Whereas steam enters and exhausts from the oscillating engine as a result of the inclination of the cylinders, with the slide valve the cylinders remain static.

This example of a North Sea Drifter, once a common sight around the shores of Great Britain was seen at the Model Engineer Exhibition, It is powered by a single cylinder slide valve engine. Model built by Harry Eastick. (Photo - Neal Read)

The single cylinder slide-valve engine used to power the steam drifter shown on the previous page.

Bolted to the cylinder port face is a rim, known as the steam chest, over which in turn is bolted a cover; gaskets ensure that the set up is steam tight. As with the oscillator, the port face contains the ports but instead of being side by side they are in line and the one used for exhaust is larger than the one that acts as an inlet. A separate valve controls steam distribution and this has a recess in it, the purpose of which we will come to shortly. The movement of the valve is controlled by an eccentric that is attached to the crankshaft, and passes through the wall of the steam chest, via a steam proof gland.

Steam is allowed into the steam chest and the rotation of the eccentric moves the valve clear of the inlet port allowing steam into the cylinder, the valve is of course at that stage sealing the exhaust port. As the piston starts to move, so does the valve and it initially seals both inlet and exhaust ports, but as the piston reaches the end of its stroke, the valve opens the exhaust port. It would not be any use the spent steam exhausting into the steam chest to join the fresh steam waiting to be used and this is why there is a recess in the valve. The spent steam passes into the recess and from there can escape to atmosphere. The valve continues its movement and again opens the inlet covering the exhaust and the whole cycle starts again.

Single acting slide valve engines have their place when headroom is limited but most slide valve engines are double acting as unlike the oscillating engine not a great deal more space is required for a double acting engine than for a single one. For a double acting engine the port face contains three ports, two are inlet and the central one is for exhaust. The steam cycle is much the same; except that now the valve covers two ports instead of one and exhaust steam is taken out via the same port that it went in and through the recess in the valve is transferred to the exhaust port. Unlike the inlet valves the exhaust has no connection at all with the cylinder bore, the steam is just transferred through the valve.

With an oscillating engine reversal is by moving steam from one port to the other, the directional rotation of the slide valve engine is governed by the position of the piston when steam is admitted. This in turn is controlled

Principle of the slide valve.

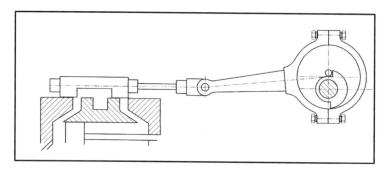

by the position of the eccentric, mostly a valve gear of some sort will be fitted that enables the operator to make the change. (See Chapter 14) As we will see there are various types of valve gear that can be used and in addition to reversing the engine some will control the steam flow, by cutting it off before the piston has reached the end of its stroke, this allows the expansion properties of the steam to be used to better advantage. The use of cut-off was common with steam locomotives but is unlikely to be of use in a model boat.

Except in special circumstances that do not really apply to marine engines the valve is made just slightly larger than the distance between the ports to ensure that when it covers them steam cannot escape through the wrong hole. If it was made to the exact size there is always the danger of a small gap appearing. This extra length is called lap: lap and lead are frequently discussed with great authority by steam buffs that tend to shroud the terms in mystery, but lap is nothing more than that, a little increase on the size of the valve to prevent steam from absconding.

Another mystery word talked about in hushed tones is lead, which when it comes down to it is a very simple thing. When the valve is set it needs to be opened for the steam to get in, more or less when the piston is at the end of the cylinder. In that way the steam does the maximum of work as it is filling the cylinder as the piston is forced down. Lead is simply the fact that as a rule steam is actually admitted minutely in advance or in the lead of the piston arriving at the end of the cylinder, more or less so that it can start its work the

split second the piston is ready to start moving. The amount of lead even on a full sized engine is very small and on models such as we are thinking of it is really a very tiny amount, so don't be fooled by any talk about the amount of lap and lead. There must be a bit of lap, that is pure common sense but the amount of lead is so small that there is no need to worry about it. At the same time it will be necessary for the port to open at the moment the piston is about to start work.

As lead has been mentioned above this might be the time to refer to valve

A small slide valve engine, combined with a vertical boiler, leaving plenty of spare room in the boat.

A twin cylinder slide valve engine made from castings, most model engineering suppliers stock a range of these.

settings, even though we have not yet got through the construction of the engine. It is simple enough, the steam port must be cracking open by about the thickness of a cigarette paper when the piston is at top dead centre and the same at the other end of course.

Guide bars

A major difference between slide valve engines and oscillating ones is the necessity to have some means of ensuring the piston remains straight in the bore. With the oscillating engine the cylinder tilts at the same angle as the piston rod and so the two automatically remain in line. The slide valve and other types of fixed cylinder engine have rigid cylinders and the piston is brought into line to slide up and down the cylinder, via a joint with a connecting rod. Part of the thrust of that rod comes at an angle and so is tending all the time to move the piston sideways in the bore. With a double acting engine there is always the bottom gland to assist in keeping the piston in line, this is insufficient to counteract the sideways thrust and in no time at all the gland would be worn to form a slot. This is a situation that is not desirable in any form of engine, be it single or double acting.

To rectify this, a guide is necessary which mostly takes the form of guide bars, sometimes referred to as slide bars, because the piece that connects the piston and connecting rod, which is known as the crosshead, slides along them. The bars take a variety of forms, they can be double with the crosshead, sliding between them, or they can be a single bar with some means of allowing the crosshead to slide along it. Yet another alternative is to use a tube like affair, generally known as trunk, in which case the crosshead slides inside it. The guide bars are very important and when building an engine it is essential that they are adequate to offer the required support. They also need to be reasonably substantial as there can be considerable sideways pressure imparted by the piston rod, particularly as wear takes place.

Making guide bars and the necessary crosshead

to fit them calls for considerable accuracy and any misalignment will result in a tight spot on the engine. If two bars are used the distance between them must be even throughout their length and whether two or a single bar is used it is essential that they are absolutely parallel to the line of the bore of the cylinders.

In the case of launch type engines, that are mounted on pillars it is not unusual for the guide bars to be dispensed with and to place the pillars, supporting the cylinders exactly on the centre lines of the cylinders and to use the pillars to act as guides by simply extending the crosshead to run between them. This also means that there can be a certain amount of reduction in the height of the engine, the crosshead can travel as far down the pillars as one wishes.

There is actually a way of avoiding the use of guide bars altogether and as some people find them difficult to make so that they are a good fit, this alternative is worth considering. Quite simply all that is required is to extend the piston rod right through the piston and out the other end. It must also extend beyond the end cover, which is then fitted with a gland similar to the one where the piston rod usually enters the cylinder. The piston rod is now supported at each end and there can be no sideways movement, because it has to pass through both glands. As well as being an easy way out, as an additional bonus there can be a considerable saving in height as the length allowed for the guide bars is no longer required. An engine built in this manner looks attractive when running with the visible rods moving in and out.

Like the oscillating engine it is possible to buy an engine with slide valves and in addition there are various kits available. These follow the trend going from basic castings through the various stages to completely machined parts that just have to be assembled. Most are on the large side and if an engine is required to suit a particular boat then the only thing to do is to make it oneself.

Engine construction

The techniques used to make a slide valve engine are not very different from those used for oscillating engines. Unlike the oscillator the ports will be in the centre of the port face and there is no port block. The steam chest can be fabricated by using strips of brass of rectangular section. One of the most difficult parts is in the need to transfer the steam from the port face to the cylinder bore, which generally requires accurate drilling of small holes, although there are ways to avoid doing this.

Most commercially made drawings will show the steam and exhaust ports as slots and in the case of very large cylinders this is the correct way to go about it. It is hard to imagine an engine that is being put in a model boat that will need to have them slotted, ordinary plain drilled holes will be quite sufficient and the recess in the valve, which is usually shown as square can be round. Trying to make a square recess is far from easy unless milling equipment is available and a square one will not work any better than the round one.

Cylinders

The idea of using a length of round tube, soldered to a piece of flat section for making cylinders will work with slide valve engines although it is more usual to make the cylinder from solid bar, unless of course castings are being used. The easiest material to use is square as the port face is already present and once the ports have been added needs no more than a rub on some abrasive paper. Cylinder covers can be soldered in place but it is preferable that they are bolted, this allows the piston

position to be seen when the valves are being set, rather than having to rely on the crank setting. It is nice to be able to see the exact point at which the piston reaches the top of its stroke.

There should be a minimum of four points of fixing for the covers, to copy full sized practice they should be secured with studs and nuts, with exactly one and a half thread turns showing when the nut is tightened. In full sized practice the figure four would have been much more likely to be twenty-four, but most will not want the bother of going to such lengths. The diameter of the studs to be used may be cause for some concern, 10BA or 1.4mm can be used for a 3/8 in. or 10mm bore cylinder, anything smaller will need to be held in place with 12BA studs.

It is not a lot of fun tapping large numbers of 12BA holes, in a piece of bronze and the way to avoid doing so is to drill clearance sized holes. Snip the heads of some 12BA bolts and

Cyril the model launch made by Malcolm Beak and with which he carried out a large number of experiments. It is driven by the small twin cylinder slide valve engine, full drawings of which were supplied by Malcolm and are reproduced on pages 50 -52.

Proteus - a commercially produced twin cylinder slide valve engine with valves operated by eccentrics on a gear-driven layshaft.

the ends and then solder the port face to the cylinder, ensuring the solder does not fill the grooves. Before soldering it in position, drill the cylinder block from the position of the grooves into the bore, finally rub down the new port face.

Steam chest

The steam chest can be fabricated from strip, soldering the ends after ensuring the joints are square. That too will need to be well rubbed down on abrasive paper so as to try and ensure its accuracy while soldering is nearly impossible and although a gasket will be fitted unless the chest is flat, it will be difficult to keep steam tight. The hole to accept the gland for the piston rod should be drilled with the assembly in the four jaw chuck in the lathe is possible, this being the most accurate method of doing so. The chest has to be bolted to the cylinder block and to be correct this too should be held with nuts and studs, so why not use the same idea that was suggested for the cylinder covers?

Crankshafts

Crankshafts are made in exactly the same way as those for any other type of engine and assuming that the engine is to have more than one cylinder and therefore needs a crankshaft with a double throw, it will be best to fabricate it. It can of course be machined from solid bar but with such small diameters involved it requires very sharp tools to prevent it from buckling under the strain.

It will depend on the web thickness as to how the parts are to be assembled, with webs as thin as 1/16in or 1.5 mm

then put the shanks in the clearance holes, having first of all applied a little retaining compound. Once that is dry it will be just as secure as threaded holes and a lot less bother to do.

Ports

Another problem is in connecting the steam ports to the cylinder ends. The time-honoured way is to file a flat on the end of the cylinder bore and drill from there to meet the bottom of the port. It is not at all a difficult proposition with a cylinder bore of a couple of inches and a nice large slotted steam port. It is a bit trickier when using a 1/32" or 1.2mm drill, or perhaps even smaller, trying to break into the port that is about the same size. It can be done of course and plenty of people no doubt do, lesser mortals need a bit of assistance. The way to do it is to make a separate port face, make grooves on the underside from the ports to near it will be best to solder them together, although it does not have to be silver solder a good soft solder joint should be adequate. Webs that are thicker than that, especially if the shaft and journals are of a larger diameter can be assembled with a retaining compound.

Big-end bearings

The bearings have to be split and it is best to build them up by soft soldering two lengths of square or rectangular bar together, depending on the size of bearing required. Cut to length and square off the ends and then drill and tap the holes for the bolts that will hold the bearings together. Use the four-jaw chuck to drill the bearing holes and to drill and tap the hole for the connecting rod, then separate the two parts. Once again it would be correct to use studs and nuts for assembly and the trick of holding the studs in place with retaining compound will save tapping the holes.

Main bearings

Main bearings can be manufactured in exactly the same way as the big end bearings, with the addition of holes for bolting them to the bedplate, an oil hole should be drilled in each to ensure good lubrication.

In general terms the above describes methods that can be used to make engines, there are other ways and no doubt some readers will have their own methods of dealing with situations, however perhaps the above notes will give some guidance to those who have never tackled such tasks before.

Two Cylinder Slide Valve Engine Design by Malcom Beak

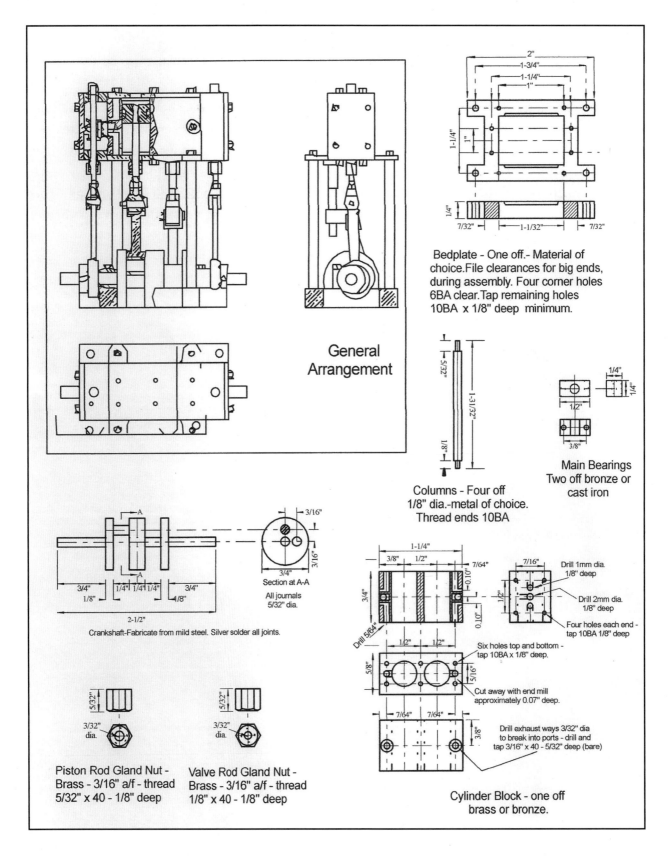

General Arrangement

Bedplate - One off.- Material of choice. File clearances for big ends, during assembly. Four corner holes 6BA clear. Tap remaining holes 10BA x 1/8" deep minimum.

Columns - Four off 1/8" dia.-metal of choice. Thread ends 10BA

Main Bearings Two off bronze or cast iron

Section at A-A
All journals 5/32" dia.

Crankshaft-Fabricate from mild steel. Silver solder all joints.

Piston Rod Gland Nut - Brass - 3/16" a/f - thread 5/32" x 40 - 1/8" deep

Valve Rod Gland Nut - Brass - 3/16" a/f - thread 1/8" x 40 - 1/8" deep

Drill 1mm dia. 1/8" deep

Drill 2mm dia. 1/8" deep

Four holes each end - tap 10BA 1/8" deep

Six holes top and bottom - tap 10BA x 1/8" deep.

Cut away with end mill approximately 0.07" deep.

Drill exhaust ways 3/32" dia to break into ports - drill and tap 3/16" x 40 - 5/32" deep (bare)

Cylinder Block - one off brass or bronze.

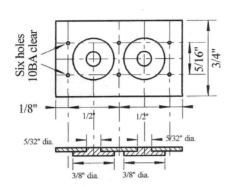

Six holes
10BA clear

5/16"
3/4"

1/8"

1/2" 1/2"

5/32" dia. 5/32" dia.

3/8" dia. 3/8" dia.

Top Cylinder Cover -
one off - 16 gauge brass sheet -
solder plugs in position.

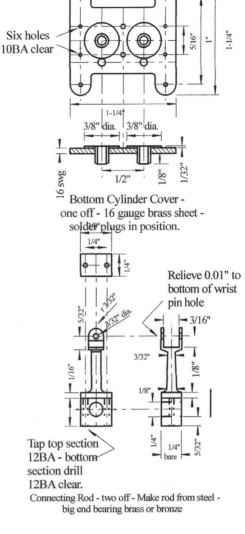

1"

Six holes
10BA clear

5/16"
1"
1-1/4"

1-1/4"

3/8" dia. 3/8" dia.

16 swg

1/2" 1/8" 1/32"

Bottom Cylinder Cover -
one off - 16 gauge brass sheet -
solder plugs in position.

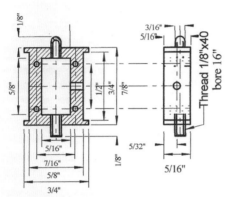

1/8"

3/16"
5/16"

5/8"

1/2"
3/4"
7/8"

Thread 1/8"x40
bore 16"

5/16"
7/16"
5/8"
3/4"

5/32"

1/8"

5/16"

Steam Chest - one off each hand -
brass with bronze bushes

1/4"

1/4"

5/32"
3/32"
3/32" dia.

1/16"

1/8"

1/4"
bare

Relieve 0.01" to
bottom of wrist
pin hole

3/16"

3/32"

1/8"

1/8"

1/4"
5/32"

Tap top section
12BA - bottom
section drill
12BA clear.

Connecting Rod - two off - Make rod from steel -
big end bearing brass or bronze

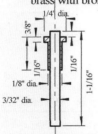

1/4" dia.

3/8"

1/16" 1/16"

1/8" dia.

3/32" dia.

1-1/16"

Crosshead Guide Assembly
Brass body - solder to bottom
cylinder cover. Stainless steel
or nickel silver secured in body
with retaining compound.

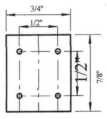

3/4"
1/2"

1/2"
7/8"

Steam Chest Cover -
two off - 1/6" brass

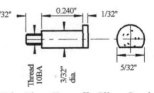

3/32" 0.240" 1/32"

Thread
10BA

3/32"
dia.

5/32"

Wrist Pin - Two off - Silver Steel

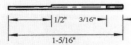

1/2" 3/16"

1-5/16"

Valve Spindles - two off - stainless steel
or nickel silver !/16" dia. - File flat for
valve nut to length 1/2" - thread other
end 10 BA for length of 3/16"

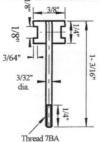

1/8"
3/8"

1/8"

1/4"

3/64"

3/32"
dia.

1-3/16"

1/4"

Thread 7BA

Piston/Rod Assembly -
two off - rod stainless
steel - piston bronze

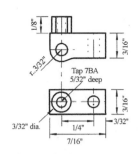

Crosshead - two off -
bronze or cast iron

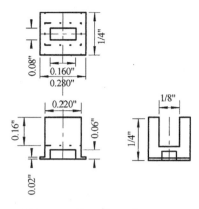

Valves - two off - cast iron or bronze

Piston Rod Gland Nut -
Brass - 3/16" a/f - thread
5/32" x 40 - 1/8" deep

Valve Rod Gland Nut -
Brass - 3/16" a/f - thread
1/8" x 40 - 1/8" deep

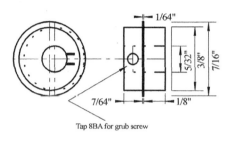

Tap 8BA for grub screw

Eccentrics - two off - mild steel

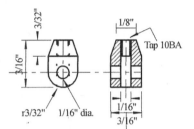

Valve Spindle Fork End -
Two off - brass

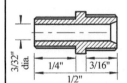

Inlet and Exhaust Stubs and Spacers - four off - brass

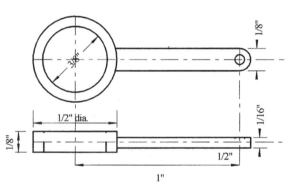

Eccentric Strap and Rod - two off -
strap - bronze: rod - hard brass -
silver solder parts together

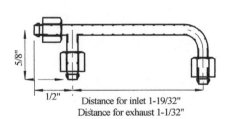

Distance for inlet 1-19/32"
Distance for exhaust 1-1/32"

Inlet and Exhausts Manifolds - one off each-
use 1/8" o/d copper pipe - silver solder all joints

6
Other Valves and Compounding

Oscillating and slide valve engines are by far the most common types that are used for model marine purposes; piston valves closely follow these. There are many other types but mostly they are generally not practical for small boats. With a couple of minor exceptions most of the other types of valves are unsuitable, because of the difficulty involved in scaling them to size. Many were tried for full size marine work but generally did not find favour, this should not stop anyone wishing to build an engine that is a bit different from so doing, there is plenty of information available on these more obscure valves. Most of these valves also require something unusual in the way of valve gear, which is another factor that makes them unsuitable.

Piston valve engines
In full size practice the slide valve eventually gave way to the piston valve, as it was generally more efficient, something that is not necessarily so in model form as it is essential that a piston valve is a good fit, whereas with a slide valve operating in a steam chest minor inaccuracies have slightly less effect. This does not mean that slide valves should not be made with care, it is just that there is a certain amount more flexibility when they are used. Nevertheless a well made piston valve

is more efficient than a well made slide valve and to anyone with even a small amount of experience in machining they are worth considering.

To ensure absolute concentricity the valve bobbin or piston should be machined from an oversized piece of material and the bore for the piston rod made with the same lathe setting as the outside diameter. Contrary to what one may believe, three-jaw lathe chucks are rarely, or perhaps we could

A twin cylinder piston valve engine, from stock materials. The engine is also an example of dispensing with guide bars by fitting glands at the end of the cylinders. Also shown overleaf.

53

a loss of steam. That steam might escape through the exhaust, but then again it may actually enter the cylinder bore and cause unwanted back pressure.

As well as machining the piston at one setting, care must be taken to remove all burrs and it should be carefully lapped into the bore, using a mild abrasive such as brass polish, do not be tempted to use a heavy grinding paste. Lapping the two is a job that calls for patience and hurrying it by applying a coarser grinding paste than that suggested, will only result in disaster.

One advantage of the piston valve in model form is that it is possible to reverse the engine without the use of a valve gear. Normally the steam is admitted to the cylinders from outside the ends of the valve and the exhaust goes via the middle section. If the direction of the steam flow is reversed and steam admitted from the inside, then the engine will run in the opposite direction. The whole business is known as inside and outside admission, a term that is quite commonly used and the change of direction by the steam can easily be arranged with a simple valve of the type shown as a reversing valve for oscillating engines.

say almost never absolutely accurate and drilling a hole in a piece of round bar will result in an off centre hole, even if the amount is so minute that it is not easily visible with the eye. Such slight discrepancies will result in minute gaps between the valve and bore, resulting in

Poppet valves

For some reason poppet valves never gained the popularity with steam engineers that they probably deserved. A well-made valve will be absolutely steam tight and therefore is about as efficient as one can get. They are particularly useful in a single acting engine; it is when it comes to double acting ones that the difficulties arise. The most common way of operating them with a double acting engine is

To reverse a piston valve engine without valve gear, the direction of the steam flow is changedby moving the valve that is located in a recess across the steam passages.

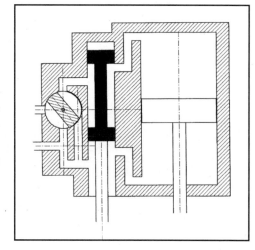

to fit a cam between the two valve stems; this can be operated either in a rotary motion or an oscillating one. Adjustment of these even in full sized practice was very difficult indeed and is something of a nightmare when miniaturised. Mushroom-headed valves can be replaced with balls and operated with pushrods, in that form they are much easier to make and to get steam tight.

Poppet valves are normally operated by either a cam or an eccentric fitted to the crankshaft, allowing fine adjustments to be made, the linkage from there goes to the cam in between the valve rods. A variation on this method of operation is the so-called clapper engine. This type of engine operates via a poppet valve that is pushed from its seat by the piston, unlike the normal poppet valve which is spring loaded for return, the clapper valve relies on steam pressure. The result is a distinct sound that is made as the valve closes, hence the name clapper valve. Most clapper valve engines only work at quite high speeds, they are very easy to make and can be used in a boat designed for free running, as well as with the gearbox described in Chapter 12.. Because the piston operates the valve, clapper engines are only single acting. Changing the direction or rotation is by rotating the crankshaft, so they are not really suitable for model marine work, except for non-radio controlled models.

Compounding

Compounding is the name given to using the exhaust steam from one cylinder to power another, the system has been extended so that the steam was

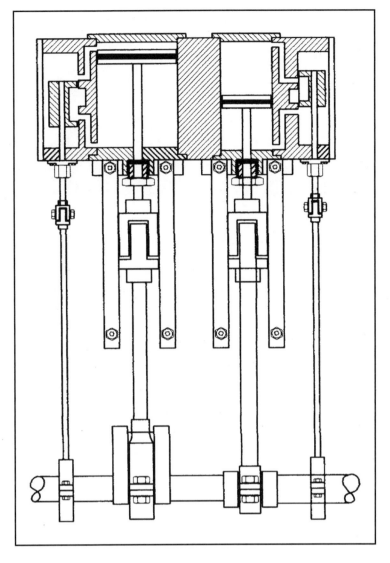

used three times and occasionally even four, but let us start at the beginning and think what will be involved in making a compound engine.

Oscillating engines

Firstly we should accept that compounding an oscillating engine in the form that it is generally modelled is not practical, this is not to say that it cannot be done and indeed there is very little more to making a compound oscillator than there is to making an ordinary two cylinder engine. The problem arises from the fact that both inlet and exhaust ports are the same size and the usual method of making a two-cylinder engine is to put inlet

In the compound engine, the exhaust from the high pressure cylinder is connected to the steam chest of the larger, low-pressure cylinder.

A compound engine built by Martin Ranson, the cylinders have been carefully lagged both for appearance and to conserve heat.

Another view of the compound engine by Martin Ranson, this time showing the complete steam plant, which is a credit to the builder.

and exhaust between the two cylinders so that live steam enters each cylinder at the same time. As the exhaust will alternate between ports depending on the direction of travel it is impossible to have one larger than the other, although it could probably be arranged for an engine that was to work in one direction only.

Oscillating engines were compounded and even made as triple expansion engines in full sized practice but they worked on a very different principle, with a separate slide valve for each cylinder. This gave each cylinder its own set of ports making the system quite workable. It is very rare indeed to see an engine of this type in model form and those that are built are invariably too large for fitting into a boat.

Non oscillating engines

Because slide and piston valve engines have their own individual valve arrangements compounding is possible. As a rule the valves and valve gear are at each end of the engine and a pipe is used to link the exhaust from the high pressure cylinder to the steam chest of the low pressure one. The exhaust from that cylinder can be disposed of as one would with a normal single or double cylinder engine. This was also a system used in full size engines.

Triple expansion

If the steam can be used twice, why not three or even perhaps four times? It most certainly was and the triple expansion engine became the most extensively used type. The quadruple expansion engine found slightly less favour, in order to get real efficiency from the very large fourth cylinder it was necessary to re-heat the steam supplied to it, this involved extra heating arrangements and generally made maintenance more difficult, which is almost certainly the reason why the system was not used more. Some triple expansion engines also had this sort of arrangement but it is unlikely to have any advantage in model form.

With a triple expansion engine one valve, including of course the valve gear will have to be set in the middle in order to operate the central intermediate cylinder, which means setting the valve without being able to see it. In addition it means that the

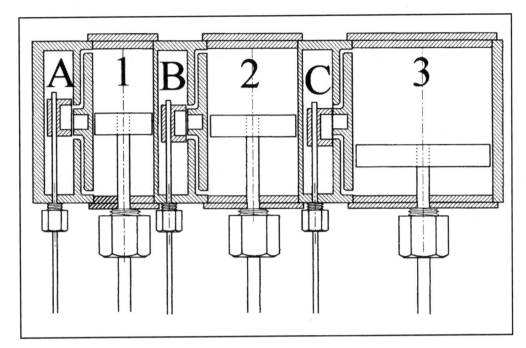

The triple expansion engine: the steam flows sequentially from the small diameter high pressure cylinder (1), through the intermediate cylinder (2) to the large bore low pressure cylinder (3).

cylinder assembly has to be assembled using long screws, or preferably studs, so that the intermediate valve chest can be assembled. It is a challenge to anyone wishing to try it and is not ideal arrangement for anyone wanting an engine small enough to put in a model boat. Triple expansion engines are very popular as models and are frequently made but usually they are far too large for a model boat and as far as is known there has not been a published design of suitable size.

Another way

There is another way to make life a little easier if one wishes to build a triple expansion engine and while it might seem a little unorthodox it is a system that has been used in full sized practice. It is to work the valves via a lay shaft arrangement. This allows the valves to be placed at the ends of the cylinders and actually makes quite an attractive arrangement. The shaft is operated with gears and runs in bearings, the assembly is bracketed to the frame of the engine. The gear ratio must of course be such that the shaft rotates at the same speed as the crankshaft and there should be an intermediate gear to ensure that both crank and valve shaft are rotated in the same direction.

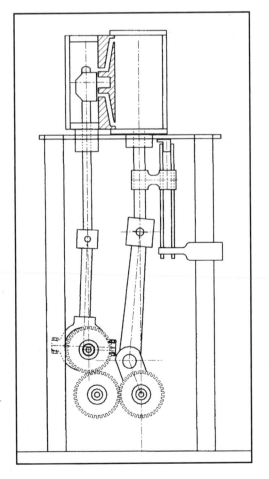

Gear driven valve mechanism to drive each individual steam valve on a triple expansion engine.

As with most multi cylindered engines the pistons are set at 90 deg.in the case of a two cylindered engine and a 120 deg. for a three cylindered type. The arrangement is designed to allow steam to push one cylinder down while at the same time driving the other up. In the case of a twin cylinder single acting engine the cranks are sometimes set at a 180 deg. as no steam will be admitted from below the pistons and only the force on top will be used. This generally will allow a smoother running engine but has its disadvantage in a boat, as it is then not reliable when it comes to self-starting, so is advisable to set the cranks at 90 deg.

Although compound and triple expansion engines always look very complicated, as indeed they usually are, a compound takes little more work than an ordinary two cylinder engine, the only difference being the additional pipe from the high pressure exhaust to the low pressure cylinder. A tripe expansion engine unfortunately will take more effort because of the necessity of getting a working valve to the centre cylinder. However for those who might be looking to make an engine that looks like an authentic triple expansion but is not too difficult to make, an engine can be made with three progressively sized cylinders. The centre or as it should be intermediate one is not fitted with either a valve or piston, the piston and valve rods are designed to work but go into empty valve chambers and cylinders. There is no need to worry about that very awkward blind valve setting, or splitting the engine, and only the constructor will know that it is not really triple expansion.

A horizontally opposed engine

For vessels with low headroom the horizontally opposed engine will solve the problem. The drawings show an oscillating engine made in that form and it will be seen that little headroom is needed; a similar arrangement-using slide or piston valve arrangements are also possible. The only complication is the fact that the pipes connecting the cylinders have to be crossed over in order to connect the two cylinders. This is easier with slide or piston valve engines, as the steam connections go to steam chests rather than ports as they do with the oscillating engine.

The frame of the engine is a length of ¾ in x 1/8 in angle. The port blocks are screwed to it. The crankshaft runs in a bearing fitted to the angle and the cylinder pivots pass through the angle, the tension spring bearing on it. The only other part that differs from a normal oscillating engine is the big end bearing or bearings. The drawings show two different versions of these and the builder can decide for him or herself which type they wish to use.

7
Boiler Making

Many modellers who would like to make their own steam plants are put off by the thought of making a boiler because of the equipment that is believed to be necessary. There is actually less equipment needed to make a boiler than there is to build an engine and making a boiler always seems to give oneself a great deal of satisfaction. Let us therefore first of all look at what we really do need to make a boiler suitable for marine use.

For a start somewhere to do the actual work is essential, it is not practical to do the job on the kitchen table without some undesirable consequences to the kitchen. On a reasonably fine day the work can be done outside in the open air, which in some ways is an ideal place to do so as during the process a certain amount of fumes will be given off and these will disperse more quickly in the open air. On the downside for this, is that it is necessary to retain the components at a high temperature for quite long periods of time and while this is easily done in the open air on a hot summer day cold air will quickly cool the work making it difficult and it can completely spoil it. Another problem associated with working in the open air, particularly in bright weather is that it is not possible to see how the temperature changes are affecting the copper and if a powerful blowlamp

is being used it is possible to cause irreparable damage. Therefore while the heat of a summer day is welcome and will assist, do make sure the work is being carried out in a shady area so that any colour changes can be seen.

Work places

The ideal place in which to work is a brick or stone built garage where the temperature can be easily maintained but it is essential to ensure a good supply of air by leaving a window open or perhaps a door ajar. Not only will doing so help to clear away any fumes, it will also ensure the supply of oxygen that is essential to maintain a good heat and to actually keep the heat supply working.

Wooden sheds can also be used but in that case the work should be done in the centre of the building and not against the walls. There will be a certain amount of radiant heat coming from the work and if it is being done against a wooden wall there is a real danger of that wall catching fire. Again it will be necessary to ensure that there is suitable ventilation for the reasons stated above. If the shed has a felt roof it is quite possible that enough heat will be generated if the boiler is a large one, to melt the bitumen in the felt. A simple precaution, such as fixing a sheet of hardboard an inch or so away from

A simple brazing hearth, utilising an old baking dish and some silicone bricks. Note the home made tongs that are used for lifting the hot boiler and quenching it, they are quite simple to make by simply twisting strips of ½ x 1/16 ins. steel to shape, in the vice, drilling a hole in each and putting either a rivet or nut and bolt through to act as a pivot.

the roof timbers will prevent this from happening. It would be most unwise to attempt the job in the loft of a house or somewhere similar, although providing reasonable care is taken there is no danger of a conflagration it is better to be safe than sorry.

The brazing hearth

Although we refer to the actual working surface as a brazing hearth, if this conjures up visions of something like a blacksmith's forge have no fear, as a simple set up will be quite adequate. Boiler making will not involve work that reaches anywhere near the temperatures required by the blacksmith or even that which is necessary for brazing, which involves heating metal to a point where a brazing rod that is really a strip of brass will melt on it. We will be using silver solder that melts at a considerably lower temperature than that and the boiler needed for a model boat is not very large so we require a relatively small area in which to work. Nevertheless a suitable hearth will be needed, albeit possibly an improvised

one, but the way it is constructed will have a considerable bearing on the ease with which a boiler can be made.

The hearth consists of a number of bricks or blocks of a suitable heatproof material in some sort of metal container and let us first of all think about the latter. It obviously must be made of metal, as it needs to be heatproof and it needs also to be supported at about waist height, unless one is content to kneel on the floor to do the job. Although it will be covered with heatproof bricks or blocks it is going to get hot and if laid directly on a wooden bench, it will at the very least get scorched if not actually burnt. Therefore it either needs an independent stand or when put on a bench should be laid on either bricks or metal blocks.

The shape of the container will no doubt depend on what is readily available, if possible it should have three folded up edges and a slightly higher back. No doubt some people will be able to make one, most will probably not have the facilities and will have to resort to something that can be adapted. The item that immediately springs to mind is an ordinary, large domestic tray and perhaps it might be possible to purchase one cheaply at a car boot sale. There are two minor disadvantages to using one, firstly they are invariably painted and when first used the paint will burn, giving off unwanted fumes, secondly the metal is generally very thin and is likely to warp under the heat. The latter will not matter too much but definitely any paint or varnish should be removed before the tray is used. Large baking trays make quite good containers for hearths and although even they can warp under the heat that is generated, the effect will be less noticeable than with an ordinary tray. Although it is proposed that fire bricks be placed round the edges, because there will be gaps where the bricks meet each other, heat will escape through, the actual loss of heat in those circumstances is less important than the consequences of anything that happens to be nearby, as it will get burned. There will be less heat escaping around the sides of the hearth and so while desirable, metal sides are less important than the metal back. The importance of having the metal back and if possible sides as well cannot be over emphasised, apart from preventing heat and flames going right through the bricks and causing damage to people or property, it also helps reflect the heat back to the working area. If all this sounds rather frightening it is not intended that way, it is simply a case of taking sensible precautions when using a flame that is considerably larger than we are ever likely to use for other purposes. In addition conservation of the heat is essential in order to get sufficient heat to the work in order to solder the boiler.

Having organised the container we now come to the bricks and they must be of the heat reflecting variety. The type of brick sold for use in domestic fireplaces is a waste of time as it will literally absorb any heat applied to it, which is not what we want at all. Most model engineering suppliers will stock suitable firebricks but if possible it is best to obtain the type used to line kilns used by potters, they are usually made of silicone and reflect about 80% of the heat applied to them. If the worst comes to the worst and a suitable supplier cannot be found then try the local builders' merchant for Thermolite bricks, while not in the same league as the silicone type, they are nevertheless pretty good and certainly a big improvement on the ordinary firebrick.

With the workplace sorted out, it is now necessary look at the actual equipment needed for making the boiler and the most obvious item is something with which to supply the heat. The ideal thing is large blowtorch working via a hose from a Propane gas cylinder, it must be attached through a special regulator, with an anti-blowback device fitted. These torches are expensive items and not everybody will feel justified in spending that sort of money, fortunately they can usually be hired from companies specialising in tool hire. It is possible to use the type of blowtorch obtainable at a builders' merchant or DIY store that has a self contained gas cylinder, two of these will be necessary so an assistant will be required and the torches must be large ones. Unfortunately they work with Butane gas, which does not give off the same amount of heat as Propane and so even with two of them it is essential that the heat be reflected back to the work as much as possible. Only trial and error will tell if the heat is sufficient.

If a second blowlamp is used, the flame should be directed at an area of the boiler that is not being worked on at that moment. The heat applied with it will graduate along the copper and ensure sufficient overall heat is available. It might be possible to make some sort of support for the second torch if nobody will volunteer to act as an assistant.

Oxy-acetylene equipment

It is surprising how many people who have access to oxy-acetylene equipment, think that will be the answer, well it may be but only if certain conditions are applied. The problem with using such equipment is that while the flame is very much hotter than can be obtained with a Propane blowlamp it is also very localised, in fact it is more or less a pinpoint. Copper absorbs heat at a very rapid rate and no sooner has a flame been applied to one area than the heat has transferred to another and because it has spread over such a large area it rapidly disappears into the atmosphere, which is of course the very reason for the advice on providing brick that will reflect the heat back again.

To use oxy-acetylene it will therefore be necessary to have a very large nozzle, somewhere in the region of 50 - 20 and in addition the boiler must be heated with a blowlamp as well, to stop the heat from just vanishing. Under those circumstances the equipment can be used quite successfully and has the advantage that it raises the temperature at a localised area preventing the solder from running all over the place as is likely to happen when just using blowlamps.

There are some folk who worry that the equipment will burn a hole in the copper but this will not happen under normal conditions because the heat will be taken away too quickly. The problem could arise however when heat is applied to thin flue tubes and to stays. These will not dissipate the heat quite so rapidly and could therefore be damaged by prolonged heating with oxy-acetylene.

Tools

Not many other tools are needed but the copper will need to be drilled in various places and a hammer will be required to form the end plates. A vice is also necessary to hold the plates while giving them a good bashing with a hammer, so it should be quite a sturdy one. Apart from those the only requirement will be for a means of picking up the hot boiler without dropping it. Possibly this could be done with stout pliers, but it is worth while spending half an hour or so making a pair of tongs to do the job. These need not be complicated and ordinary mild steel section about 3/8 x 1/8 in or 10 x 3mm will do. They are bent to the correct shape, the curved section should be a little bit smaller than the diameter of the boiler itself, a nut and bolt is put through them to act as a pivot and that is all that is required. The small amount of time required to make them will be quickly repaid by the convenience that is gained.

Construction

To make the boiler, start by ensuring the ends of the tubing are perfectly square and to the correct length. If the tubing needs to be cut to length, in order to keep the cut square, wrap a piece of insulation or masking tape round the

tube, checking of course that it is laid square, then cut along the edge of the tape. Use a nice, sharp 24 t.p.i. hacksaw blade, or in the case of very thin tubing 32 t.p.i. and above all do not try and hurry as hurrying is a recipe for disaster. When hack sawing in normal circumstances the correct method is to make a single cut right across the work. To cut large diameter copper tubing it will usually be found far easier to make a series of cuts that line up with the edge of the tape, that are about a quarter in depth of the tube thickness and having completed the circumference extend the cuts through, until the section parts. The tape will be found useful as a guide for finishing and squaring the ends with a file and should be left in place until everything is ready for soldering operations to begin.

Location of bushes

It may seem strange to someone new to boiler making to talk about bushes for fittings before the boiler is hardly started, but it is far easier to mark out and drill the holes before any form of assembly has taken place. In addition, whatever else might happen we certainly do not want to seal both ends before making some means of escape for the hot air generated by the soldering process and so now is the time to make the holes in which the bushes will fit. We need one for a safety valve, one to hold a removable cap to be used when filling the boiler, one for the regulator in the end plates and a couple in the barrel for checking the water level. The end plates also need drilling of course for any tubes that are going to be used, if the boiler is to work horizontally, the position is reversed, the regulator, etc., will be along the top and the water level bushes in one end.

Getting a straight line along the length of the tubing as a guide to the position of the holes for the bushes is not all that easy. If a rule is laid along it, almost inevitably it will slip to one side before the scriber has got half way along. There are two ways round this, either tape the rule in position with masking tape, or alternatively use a piece of angle material laid with the open vee on the boiler shell. Having marked the position of the holes for the bushes the next job is to drill them and for a start a centre punch mark should be made, the tube can be rested on a piece of wood. This should be just shaped to give support but there is no need to go mad and round it off perfectly. It is a good idea to scribe the circumference of the hole to be drilled, using a pair of dividers and the centre punch mark as a locating point, this helps to give some idea of how the finished product will look.

The drill used for the holes should be slightly blunted by rubbing a small oilstone over the cutting edges. A sharp drill will snatch at the metal as it breaks through and unless it is really clamped down tight the metal will climb up the drill and mangle not only the hole but also the surrounding metal. Putting a piece of abrasive cloth, with the abrasive side facing the cutting edge, between the drill and the metal is also a good way of preventing it snatching when it breaks through. If either of these methods is used it should be possible to complete the hole in one go; where possible when drilling copper the use of progressively larger drill should be avoided. However having said that, trying to drill a hole with a fairly large diameter drill and no pilot hole is in itself at times something of a recipe for disaster. It is impossible to stop the drill wandering even if a start has been made with a centre drill. In which case, making a small diameter hole that just breaks into the underneath of the metal and then using a countersink bit to obtain a deeper indentation also works. It is also worth putting the metal on a block of wood or probably better still a piece of chipboard in order to do the drilling as that appears to take away some of the tendency for the drill to snatch. Whichever method is going to be used the work must be securely clamped down.

A series of small holes are required around the diameter of the tube for rivets to hold the end plate in position while it is soldered and if it is to be silver soldered half a dozen or so will be plenty. Before silver soldering became the normal method of construction the rivets used to be used to hold the parts together permanently and they were spaced at a distance of one and half times their diameter. Whether the rivets are closed (hammered over) or not will depend on the position to be occupied by the flange plate. If the flanges are turned inwards the rivets cannot be closed and will be used only to hold things together during subsequent operations. In which case there is a distinct danger that during subsequent operations they will fall out and all your careful alignment of the job will have been completely wasted. The way to sort that problem out is to give the shank of each rivet a smart tap or two with the flat end of a flat pein hammer, do it somewhere near the head and the rivets will stay in place during subsequent operations. If the flanges are turned outwards, the rivets can be closed and will form part of the strength of the boiler.

Flux

The flux recommended by the manufacturer of the solder should be used and it should be mixed with water to a fine creamy paste, the addition of a couple of drops of washing up liquid to the water works wonders here as it makes it easier to paint on to the joints. Some people prefer to mix the flux with methylated spirits because when mixed with water it will occasionally boil up and run all over the work, to be followed shortly afterwards by the solder. Whether to use water or methylated spirits is a matter of personal choice, what suits one person does not necessarily suit another.

Silver soldering

The question is often asked, " Where does soldering finish and brazing begin?" There is no short answer to that, silver solders come in a wide range of specifications and each has its own melting point. In fact each has two melting points, the solidus and the liquidus; the names although

A former for swaging ends of a boiler to shape. These can be made of steel, or if only to be used once hard wood will do. The one shown is something of a compromise as it consists of ¼ in aluminium plate fastened to ½in thick chipboard it also acts as a drilling jig, for the centre flue and stays.

Latin are self explanatory, at the lower range it is thick and like a soft plastic at the liquidus state it runs everywhere, particularly to places where it is not required. It is at the latter stage that it does its job and the temperature at which it will happen will depend on the grade, but it will be anywhere 600 and 800 degrees centigrade. This is sufficient for Johnson Mathey, the main supplier of silver solder in Great Britain to call the process silver brazing, so it would appear that it can be referred to as either soldering or brazing, but whatever it is called it requires a great deal of heat.

Like all soldering operations the metal must be heated to the point where the solder will melt on it, which in the case of silver solder on copper is a dull red colour. It is no use sticking the solder in before it has turned that colour as all that will happen is that the flame from the blowlamp will melt it and it will lie in chunks on the metal, the joint will then be absolutely useless. If that happens trying to re-melt it is also a problem, because once silver

solder has melted to re-melt it requires 300 to an extra 400 psi. In all probability if only limited heating equipment is available it will not be possible to do so.

Once the joint has been soldered allow the metal to cool for a short while and then dunk it in a bucket of cold water, stand away as you do so and make sure that you are wearing safety glasses, as there will be a big splash. As soon as the metal has completely cooled, drain off any water and put the work in the acid. Some people like to put the hot boiler straight into acid, there seems to be no proof that this is any more efficient than waiting a while, neither does there appear to be any improvement in cleanliness. There is considerably more danger involved, as it is better to get splashed with hot water than with hot acid.

It is not advisable to try and complete the soldering of a whole boiler in a single stage, far better to do a piece at a time and then if a mistake should be made it may be possible to retrieve the situation. The final act will be to solder in the various bushes and a final cleaning in the acid.

Although the soldering operation described above is for the simplest type of boiler, the methods hold good for any type of boiler. Two things cause most failures, lack of cleanliness and insufficient heat, both of which are the fault of the constructor.

Making flanged plates

Before we can start putting the boiler together it is necessary to make flanged plates for the ends and assuming a round boiler without an odd shaped firebox or something like that, it will not be too much of a problem. A former is needed for each diameter and this can either be a steel blank, machined to the correct size, or if the former is only to be used for one pair of ends it could be made of hardwood and Medium Density Fibreboard has been known to be pressed into service. It must be perfectly round and should be the size of the inner diameter of the boiler tube, less twice the thickness of the material being used for the ends, and if it is the odd 1/32in or 1mm less than that so much the better. When making formers, holes should be drilled in the position where tubes are to be fitted, the former can then also be used as a jig for drilling those holes.

The copper for the end plates will need to be soft in order to form it to shape. Cut a piece of the end material roughly ¾ ins. or 20mm larger than the diameter of the former, take it to the hearth and heat it until it turns the colour of a boiled carrot, making sure the colour is even all over, by moving the blowlamp around, as soon as the temperature has been reached put it in a bucket of cold water. This will help to give it an initial cleaning as well as helping the softening process.

Put it centrally over the former, pop it in the vice and start hammering over the edges, go right round bending a little at a time. Trying to get one section right over and then the next will only end in disaster, as the copper will be hardening all the time it is being hit (it is called work hardening). It is going to require several sessions for which it will require re-heating before it will get to its final shape. When the work starts to get harder it is time to soften the copper again and the process started again. Doing this has the effect

of hammering unclean sections into the material and therefore it should be cleaned before doing the next stage.

Cleaning copper

The only way to get the copper clean is to put it in an acid solution and there are various thoughts on what that solution should be, nitric acid; sulphuric acid and caustic soda all have their devotees. All have the same big disadvantage, that is the fact that they are very difficult to dispose of when they are finished with. An alternative that does just as good a job, without the problem is citric acid, which can be tipped down the drain or on the garden when finished with and will do no harm. It is made by dissolving

The softened copper is now put in the vice for forming. Work gradually round and re-soften when necessary. Use a soft hammer to prevent too much marking.

After three re-heatings the plate is nearing the point where the flange is at ninety degrees to the face.

be necessary to trim any jagged pieces off to give a nice smooth finish.

Any holes in the plates that might be needed should be made and fairly small ones can be done with the drilling machine. Larger holes should always be bored when possible as this gives a much more accurate hole than drilling which often results in holes that are not completely round, particularly when they are made in sheet metal.

Assembling

Once satisfied that the flanged plates are fitting correctly it is time to assemble the boiler, any internal tubes should be fitted together with the shell and ends. To prevent movement during the soldering process it will be necessary to put rivets through the shell and into the flanges of the plates, the holes for these will have been drilled in the shell and can be transferred to the flange plates.

Any tubes should be a good push fit in their relevant holes, if they are inclined to slip out open the ends a little to stop them doing so. If they come half way out during the soldering operation life will become very difficult, as the set up will be too hot to push them back and frequently the expansion of the metal will make it impossible to do so. When satisfied with the assembly put the whole thing in the acid and when thoroughly clean, give it a quick rinse in clean water. Citric acid will not stop the soldering process if not washed away but it is better to be safe than sorry. Any bushes that are to be fitted should also be cleaned in the acid and then washed. There will be no need for further cleaning than that done by the acid.

Before the parts can be joined together it is necessary to drill any holes that are required in the flange plates. Holes for a centre flue boiler must be accurately bored . The flange plate is fixed to a block of wood with screws. At the same setting the outer edges of the flanges can be machined to obtain a good close fit in the tube.

about four tablespoons in a bucket of water and stirring vigorously, until the crystals are dissolved. It does not work quite as quickly as the more potent brews but is a lot safer and it is even possible to put ones hand in it and not suffer any ill effects.

The end plates should be left in the acid for a day or so and when bright again, repeat the process of heating – quenching and hammering, until the flanges are square to the face. There will be ripples left on the flanges and the edges will be uneven, but this is of no consequence. The flanges will have to be carefully attended to until they are a good close fit in the boiler tube, some prefer to do this in the lathe, and a great deal here will depend on the size of the machine, others are happy to file the edges.

The fact that the ends are uneven will not matter providing the flange is to be turned inwards in the shell. Some people prefer to have the flange towards the end of the shell rather than turned inwards and in this case it will

Silver soldering

All is now ready for silver soldering, which can be done with No.2 solder; this has the lowest melting point of all the silver solders. The soldering has to be done in stages but do not worry about work that has been done previously coming undone as has already been explained, once the solder has melted some of the ingredients have been boiled off and it will require a much greater temperature to re-melt it. This is also a very good reason to get things right first time round as trying to disassemble parts that have been silver soldered together is very difficult and in the case of a mass of copper can be considered as impossible.

The section that is to be soldered first of all should be fluxed, as once it is at the liquidus stage silver solder has a habit of flowing everywhere and is difficult to control, the running can be stopped by putting a heavy lead pencil line round any areas where the solder is not wanted. Any bushes should be pushed home after having flux applied to them and these will benefit from a lead pencil line drawn round them about 1/8 ins. or 3mm from the edge to stop solder flowing out.

Once all is prepared, the boiler is heated until it starts to turn a very dull red colour and the solder can then be applied to all the joints. It must melt on the copper and not be melted by the flame of the burner. That will result in blobs forming instead of the solder running into the joints. When satisfied that the solder has been properly applied allow the work to cool for a while and then dunk it in a bucket of cold water. A plastic bucket can be used for this with perfect safety because as

soon as the copper strikes the water the temperature will drop to one that will not melt the plastic. When cold, use a clean paint brush and clean water to remove as much of the discolouration as possible, the boiler should be returned to the acid and when thoroughly clean again rinsed in cold water ready for the next soldering operation.

The completed boiler should be tested to twice its working pressure and the set up used for this consists of nothing more than a simple hand pump, which is easily made and a pressure gauge of about 2 ins, or 50mm diameter. The latter can be taken from a car foot pump or it may be possible to purchase one from a scrap metal merchant. It needs

The parts assembled and held securely together, and the joint positions liberally fluxed. Note that broken brick has been placed all around the assembly in order to conserve heat .

A short length of angle is good for marking positions of bushes, it can be of any metal. The necessary bushes can then be soldered in place.

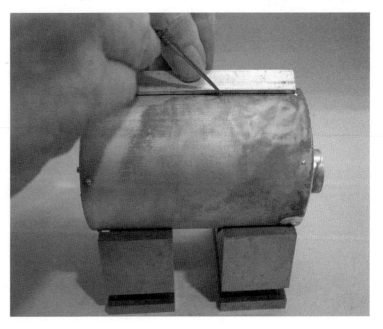

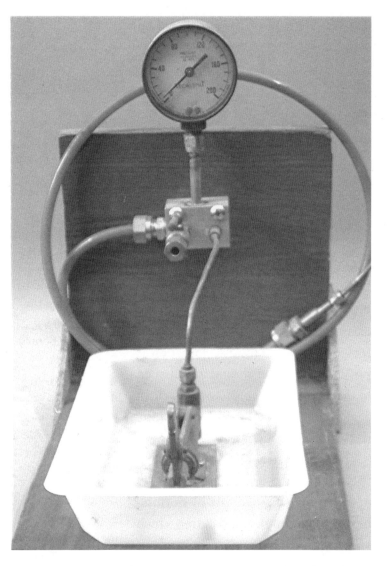

Picture shows a typical rig for boiler testing.

pressure is reached. It takes very little to build up the pressure and while it is essential to get the test pressure right, a single extra stroke of a pump will raise it much higher very quickly.

The pressure should be maintained for at least a quarter of an hour. If it shows any sign of dropping use the pump to keep it up. Let it down slowly by half releasing a plug and then examine the boiler for any distortion, don't worry about leaks. A leak is not dangerous; a boiler will not fail because of one and in fact until the advent of welded boilers all full size ones used to leak. Any minor leaks therefore can be ignored, if there is a major one or lots of small ones, it is probable that it will be possible to repair them by applying more solder so all is not lost. The odd tiny pinprick will seal itself when the boiler is in use and need not be worried about.

Members of clubs may have to have their boilers tested by club officials but it is as well to test for oneself before taking them along to be tested officially.

Clothing

Before closing the chapter on boiler making a word or two about self-protection will not come amiss. Good quality cotton or leather gloves should be worn during all soldering operations, we are looking at the use of temperatures in excess of 600 degrees centigrade and just getting near to the work can cause burns on the hands. Avoid the use of man made fibres in general clothing, while we are not getting near to the temperature in a foundry things are going to get very hot. Foundry workers are forbidden to use

to be reasonably accurate but absolute accuracy is not that important. All bushes must be plugged except two, the pump is to be fitted to one of these and the other, which is used for filling *must* be at the highest point on the boiler. If necessary lay the boiler on its side in order that a suitable position can be found. Fill the boiler until the water is at the very top and allow time for any air bubbles to come through, it is essential that when tested there is no air in the boiler. Once satisfied that all air has gone, plug the filler hole, connect the pump, (which should have its own water supply) and give a single stroke, see what the pressure is and then give one or more strokes until the required

A side view of the completed boiler.

An end view of the completed boiler.

any clothing made with synthetic fibres because of the danger they might melt and in doing so stick to the skin, so it is a wise precaution not to wear them. Safety glasses should be worn, no explosive substances are involved but although very unlikely, a drop of water remaining in the boiler after washing could have the effect of shooting out as a small jet of steam. Usually any remaining water just quickly vaporises and within seconds of the heating process starting, all traces of water will have been removed. Water will be liable to shoot up when the boiler is placed in the cold water and it is therefore sensible to protect ones eyes.

Modern silver solders are not made with toxic chemicals and so in theory a mask is not required. In fact it is wise to wear one anyway. It could be that the silver solder that has been acquired is of an old type that contains cadmium and other such chemicals, and in addition the dry heat created by the soldering process tends to dry out ones throat. A facemask will help to prevent this from happening. Finally consider wearing a hat of some sort, particularly if you have long hair. Hair is very combustible and there is an obvious danger when bending over red-hot copper, it is better to be safe than sorry.

69

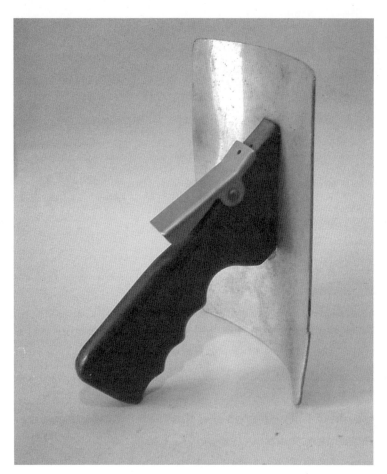

The heat involved in soldering a boiler can be uncomfortable, making it difficult to apply the solder. A shield such as this allows for the solder to be fed through it; the wooden handle provides additional heat insulation.

8

Boiler Design

Steam pressures

No matter how well designed and made a steam engine is, if the boiler is not also properly designed and of a suitable size, the engine will never run at its best. However for various reasons there will need to be some compromises when it comes to making it. The boiler is going to have to be of a size suitable to fit neatly in the boat without being obtrusive and yet at the same time capable of generating sufficient steam to drive the boat at a reasonable speed for a reasonable period of time, although it may well be possible to replenish the water supply during operations. The construction of the boiler also needs to be within the capabilities of the person attempting to build it. The beginner to model engineering, which after all is what making a steam plant is, should start with something simple, that while possibly not quite having the efficiency of a more complicated type, can at least be finished with the skill and equipment available.

The boiler has to be constructed so that it is safe at a steam pressure higher than that at which it will be required to operate, but there is absolutely no need whatever for that pressure to be extreme. There is little point in using pressures above about 30p.s.i. or around 2 bar in the average boat, nothing is to be gained by using anything higher.

We do see boats with engines working at pressures of 50psi or 4bar and even higher than that, it may be that the engine has been badly designed, or badly made and simply cannot do the job properly with a lower pressure but it is more likely the owner of the boat just simply may not realise that there is no advantage to be gained with such a high pressure. Some commercial engines are designed to allow the use of high pressures, and this is fine because it shows the engine is capable of withstanding them. Because the engine and boiler have been designed that way it does not mean that it is necessary to operate at that pressure. As long as the plant will drive the boat at a suitable speed, then that is the pressure to work at, plus possibly a little in reserve, but not much. If the boiler is operating at a high pressure and the engine has to run with the regulator partially open, there is a waste of valuable heat. If as a result of the extra pressure in the boiler the safety valves keep blowing off, something is wrong and the heat to the boiler should be reduced to a level where there is a balance between the power output required and the boiler pressure. If the pressure is such that the engine has to run with the regulator partly closed, this defeats the object of having it in the first place. It is not like a model steam road vehicle or locomotive, where additional injection of steam may be needed to cope with a gradient or an extra load. The only possible advantage a higher pressure will give in a boat is a bit of additional speed and who wants to see a Clyde Puffer sailing around like, "Bluebird"?

If a boat were to be designed for racing, higher pressures would be an advantage, but they should be used with an engine designed to run at a higher speed than would normally be expected. This was the case in full size and it follows that it is the principle that needs to be used in model form. In most instances an engine to work at high speed needs to be single acting with a short stroke.

To give a practical example that will put the working pressure in perspective we should look at our colleagues who like to build model passenger hauling locomotives. A small two cylinder 2½in gauge locomotive will usually have ½in or 12mm bore cylinders and work at around 50 psi and at that pressure it will haul the driver and a passenger, which amounts to a possible average weight of eighteen stone, in addition to the trolley on which they will be sitting. There is also a considerable frictional drag from the passenger vehicle, the power required to drive even a large boat is a mere fraction of that and yet all too often we see boats powered by engines with larger capacity cylinders working at higher pressure, something is being wasted somewhere.

Basically a boiler consists of a tube of a given diameter with plates at either end, fitted in the top of the boiler will be bushes to hold such things as safety valves and the regulator and in one of the end plates will be a bush or bushes to enable the water level to be checked in one way or another. A basic boiler generally referred to as a pot will consist of nothing more than that and as such is an ideal project for a newcomer to this sort of work. The addition of smaller tubes will add to the efficiency of the boiler by enabling the burner to apply more heat to the water inside, or in other words increasing the heating surface.

These smaller tubes can be of two types, water or fire, and the names are self-explanatory, a water tube contains water and is arranged to come into direct contact with the heating unit or burner, while the fire tube carries extra heat inside it and so transmits additional heat in that way. To get the best of both worlds, frequently boilers are designed with each type of tubing.

There is no doubt that water tubes improve boiler efficiency, because they are directly in contact with the heat source, unfortunately because they are frequently placed below the main boiler shell, the overall height of the boiler in the boat will be increased. Whether or not this matters will depend entirely on the type of boat, but it can have its disadvantages in certain circumstances. In fact as we will see not all water tubes are necessarily below the boiler, sometimes they are used in conjunction with heat tubes, which allows the boiler to be lower in the boat.

Boilers are made to stand either vertically or horizontally, the type used depends on the boat in which they are to be used. Many though certainly not all, steam launches had vertical boilers which look attractive and are frequently finished with nice brass caps. Larger vessels would have the boilers lying horizontally in order that superstructure could be built round and over them, there would be no attempt to add any embellishments, but they would be well lagged. It may well be the case that in a model of a ship, that in full size would have had a horizontal boiler or boilers, a vertical boiler will be more convenient as it occupies less space. This leaves extra room for radio control equipment, and head room may not be of prime consideration. Whether or not to follow this practice is up to the individual and will depend on how near to scale he or she wishes to build the boat.

All too often boilers seen in model boats are very large and out of proportion with the vessel, a well designed boiler in conjunction with an efficient pump will mean that even a very small boiler will generate enough steam to drive a two-cylinder engine with a bore of 1/2in (12mm) and a similar stroke. Size will ultimately of course be dependant on the vessel in which the boiler will be housed and some builders may not be the least bit concerned as to whether the finished product looks right as long as it works. That is the way it should be in a hobby, every individual free to do his or her own thing and as long as it gives them pleasure, the end result is of no concern to other people.

Many large ships had more than one boiler, the very large ones would have quite a number and they filled the bowels of the vessel. There were several reasons why this was done; the most important being that there is a practical limit to the size of a single boiler. This was not only governed by the problems involved in trying to build one massive boiler, but also the impossibility of being able to keep supplying it with sufficient fuel, which was particularly the case when they were hand stoked with coal. Another reason, which also applies to models, is the fact that one huge boiler would not only have occupied too much upper space, it would also have tended to make the ship unstable. A series of smaller boilers kept the weight down; each could be fired individually and even closed down if less steam was needed. It would be extremely difficult to replicate all these facets in miniature and so we have to compromise.

The late Don Gordon did a considerable number of experiments with boiler design and advocated making one scale or near scale boiler and non working models of the others He certainly managed to operate boats while using very small boilers, but sadly died before he was able to publish the full results of his work. However what is known of it has lead the way in the use of reasonable sized boilers and we can use his research as well as that of others to get proportions near to the right size. It is quite possible to link small boilers together to give a near scale appearance but it may not be necessary to do so. One boiler may be quite sufficient, not many model boats will be travelling from England to Australia and the others can be dummies, possibly housing the pump or some of the radio control gear. Nor would a dummy boiler need to be made of copper, it can be fabricated to appear the same as the working one, using brass or steel, thus saving both expense and working time.

With a small launch, of the type once so popular on our lakes and rivers, that had a small vertical boiler it is possible it can be built very close to scale. The boiler would generally consist of the main barrel, with a series of vertical tubes, to assist in the passage of hot gases from the burner, through the water. A series of small tubes placed across one or two of the main flue tubes will allow water to pass through and so add even more to the heating surface. There were designs involving curved tubes that were made to improve efficiency, they originated from the manufacturers of steam lorries; making a model of those will be for the experienced modeller certainly they are not for a beginner.

A model boiler is most unlikely to ever have the same number of tubes as a full size one, as it is just not possible to replicate the number of tubes that a boiler might have. Even if such a model boiler were made it would be impossible to clean the tubes when this becomes necessary, as their diameter would be so small that a brush just would not fit. It is usual therefore to use fewer tubes of larger diameter. Some boiler designs have water tubes crossing the heat tubes. This increases efficiency but raises the problem that if there is a leak where one of the water tubes joins a heat tube, it is virtually impossible to repair and possibly might even mean scrapping the boiler. If these tubes are fitted it is essential to pressure test the flues before installing them in the boiler.

It is well worthwhile taking care and some thought given to the design of the boiler, as it will pay dividends when it comes to operating the boat. The aim should be for a boiler of suitable shape that has about 25% percent more capacity than is absolutely necessary to run the engine.

Differing designs

As the boiler plays such an important part in making a steam engine work it is not surprising to find out that there have been literally hundreds of different designs. All the great engineers of

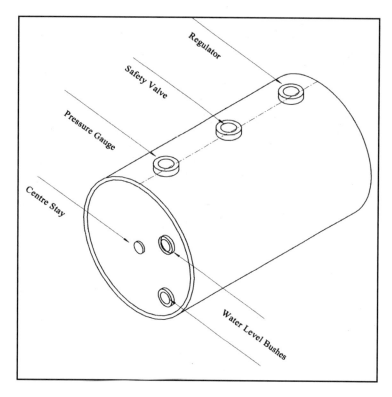

Simple horizontal pot boiler 2in dia. x 4in length from 20s.w.g. solid drawn copper tube and ends from 16s.w.g. copper sheet. One logitudanal stay from 1/4in copper. Working pressure 40p.s.i.

the late 19th and early 20th century had a try at designing a more efficient boiler and there were many successes. Most though are of no real value when it comes to model boats, being too complicated and some are designs that are just not suitable for a boat, many were never designed for marine work anyway. It is therefore proposed to only describe those considered most likely to be of use, or that the average reader is likely to be able to build with comfort and even with that limitation it is surprising just how many variations there really are. There are plenty of books describing boiler designs available for those who feel they want to try something a little different.

Pot boilers

The simplest form of boiler is known as the pot boiler and it is the easiest of all to make, although not as efficient as the more complicated types. Even quite a small one is more than capable of supplying sufficient steam to run a

single cylinder, single acting oscillating engine with a bore of 3/8in or 10mm. There appear to be two things that give regular cause for concern, the first is that occasionally people find that having made the boiler it is difficult to raise and maintain steam. Generally this is the result of using copper tube with a wall that is too thick, with the result that all the heat from the burner is being used to keep this very large piece of copper hot and very little of it is finding its way into the water. The second problem is associated with the first in as much as an inefficient or wrongly positioned burner very often causes bad steaming. A burner could be very well made and capable of supplying plenty of heat for the purpose but unless the distance between the top of the flame and the bottom of the boiler is right, it will be impossible to get good combustion and the thing just will not work.

The tip of the flame should be touching the bottom of the heating surface sufficiently to give the slightest flattening of the flame tip. If it is too close this becomes immediately obvious, as there will be a smell of fuel, be it methylated spirits or liquid petroleum gas (LPG) the result will be the same.

Testing

Boilers should always be tested and this is done by filling them with water and then pumping in some more until the pressure gauge reads twice the working pressure that the boiler is to be used at, and to do this all bushes must be plugged. That pressure should be maintained for about twenty minutes, if necessary by pumping. The boiler should then be examined for damage, which if there is any will take the form of buckled boiler plates. If the boilers have been made from the correct materials this should not happen.

If there are any leaks it will depend on their severity as to what happens, but have no fear, as a leaky boiler does not mean it is unsafe, all full sized boilers leaked somewhere or another. If the leaks amount to nothing more than a couple of pinholes, leave well alone, they will seal themselves off when the boiler is steamed. Anything more severe than that will need attention, otherwise the boiler will not maintain steam when it is in use. This either means re-soldering, or if the leak is in a suitable place, such as along the edge of the flange plates, a hole can be drilled and tapped and a length of copper rod threaded and screwed in to fill it. This is often much easier and more efficient than trying to solder over the top of the previous join. Should the boiler leak so badly that the required pressure cannot be reached, obviously severe remedial action will be needed and it may be necessary to run solder round all the joints.

Before closing on the subject there is something that should be born in mind that can cause leaks, it is cleaning the copper with an abrasive paper. This applies particularly after the boiler has been heated a time or two. The copper becomes very soft and the particles on the abrasive paper are inclined to come away as it is used and get embedded in the soft copper. The result is a number of tiny holes that are difficult to trace. So avoid the use of such material; use acid alone for cleaning, while the boiler is under construction.

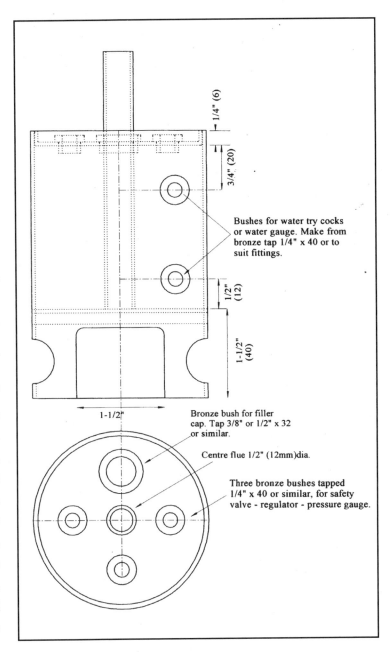

Bushes for water try cocks or water gauge. Make from bronze tap 1/4" x 40 or to suit fittings.

Bronze bush for filler cap. Tap 3/8" or 1/2" x 32 or similar.

Centre flue 1/2" (12mm)dia.

Three bronze bushes tapped 1/4" x 40 or similar, for safety valve - regulator - pressure gauge.

Simple vertical boiler

The simple vertical boiler is ideal for open launches and similar vessels and as the name suggests it is quite easy to build. There are two major differences between it and the pot boiler, apart of course from the fact that one is horizontal, the other vertical and the fact that a centre flue is included. In the case of the pot boiler it is easy enough to make arrangements for the surplus heat to escape via a chimney at one end, something that is not possible

Basic vertical boiler with 1/2in dia. centre flue. Dimmensions as shown. 3in (75mm) dia., 3in (75mm) long, 6 x 1in (25mm) dia. ventilation holes at base. Make from 18swg (1.3mm) solid drawn copper tube, silver solder all joints.

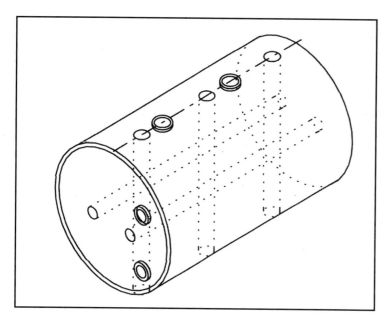

Horizontal boiler with water tubes

The horizontal boiler with water tubes below it, has been a firm favourite amongst model makers for many years, as it is a particularly good steamer. It is only a little more difficult to make than the pot boiler and to the inexperienced the only thing that might cause a problem is the tube angles. The way to deal with this is to drill the holes for the tubes and insert a length of mild steel which is then pulled in the direction at which the tube enters the boiler. The result is an angled hole into which the tube will slide.

A 3in. dia boiler with 3x vertical tubes1/4in dia. Barrel from 18s.w.g solid drawn copper tube with 2 x 3/16in dia. copper stays.

A cover with chimney is required for vertical tube boilers.

with the vertical boiler, hence the need for the flue. The other difference is the allowance at the bottom of the space for the burner; this can be made by screwing on an addition made of mild steel, some people might prefer to just use an extra length of copper tube. An opening is required for the burner and there should be a number of large holes in the skirt, as we shall call it, for air to get to the burner in order to give a good flame.

Horizontal boiler with heat tubes

There are several versions of this type of boiler, but basically it is a case of drilling holes across the barrel and inserting tubes that will conduct the heat up through the water. The tubes can be placed vertically or alternately at an angle. In the latter case they can either be arranged to emerge in line with each other, or alternately in the same formation that they entered. Any boiler made with heat tubes in this fashion should have some means of conducting the waste heat away, and this usually takes the form of a box like structure with a chimney attached. If the tubes emerge from the boiler in staggered fashion then this exhaust box will need to be wider than if they emerge in a straight line.

Vertical boiler with heat tubes

Almost identical to the simple vertical boiler but with a number of vertical tubes to conduct heat up through the

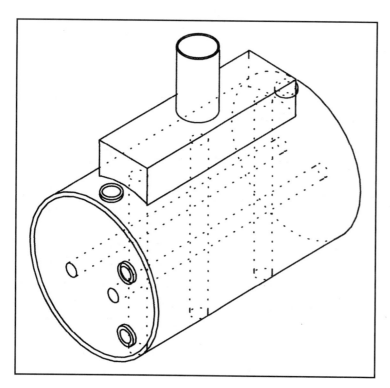

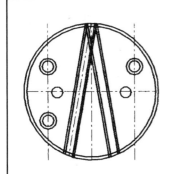 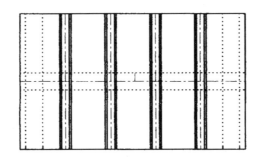 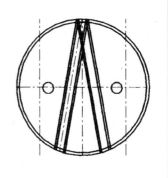

water. Like the horizontal boiler with heat tubes some form of cover will be needed to direct the heat that emerges. Therefore the centre flue does not continue up to form a chimney; an additional tube is attached to the top cover for this purpose.

Centre flue horizontal boiler

Another very popular type the boiler is basically a pot with a large centre flue, the burner being of the pencil type, the flame of which goes through the central flue. The best results obtained with it therefore are when it is used with a gas burner as the flame can be directed along the flue. This is not to say that it is never used with methylated spirit firing, and if it is to be fired in that way, a thin round burner is used. There are various ways of improving the heating capabilities of this type of boiler. When used with a gas burner heating ability can be improved by inserting a coil of nichrome wire in the flue, this is the wire that was used in old-fashioned, electric fires.

It is also possible to put cross tubes in the flue, allowing water to flow across it. Be warned that if this is done, if these tubes are not properly fitted, they might well leak and it is impossible to do anything about, so the boiler will have to be scrapped. The flue and tubes should therefore be tested before final assembly of the boiler. To do this each end must be blanked off and water pumped in to the flue tube to a pressure of at least twice the proposed boiler pressure. Any leaks will then show up and can be repaired before the boiler is finally assembled and soldered.

It is also essential that these cross water tubes are made absolutely flush with the outer edge of the flue tube, as it is essential that this is a good fit in the end plates. If the cross tubes are stranding proud it will not be possible to put the flue into the boiler ends and get a good fit.

The Marine Boiler

Always referred to as the Marine Boiler, this type was common in full sized practice and apart from the necessity to

Horizontal boiler with angled heat tubes. Construction as per vertical tube boiler. Number of tubes used is optional.

Schematic showing layout of boiler with angled tubes.

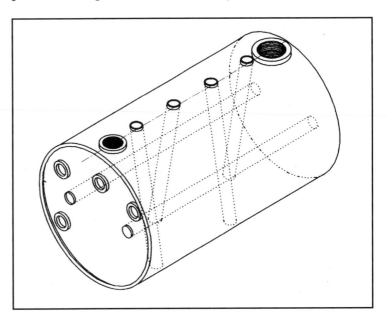

Multi-tubular vertical boiler with added heat tubes to improve efficiency. If leaks persist, it is easy to repair. Construction as per simple vertical boiler.

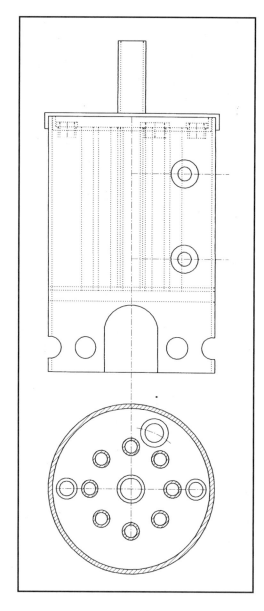

A commercially made boiler from Cheddar Models.

reduce the number of flue tubes, because of their size, it can be modelled more or less exactly. It has a large tube in which the heating is carried out (that extends between a third and half the length of the barrel), from there a series of flue tubes extend to the end of the barrel. The only difficulty with it is the limited room in the firebox.

Horizontal boiler with flue tubes

Not a very difficult boiler to make and yet considerably more efficient than the plain pot boiler described on page 74, for those with the facilities to make it and who require a horizontal boiler it is recommended. It is actually something of a hybrid as it incorporates ideas from two types. One of these is something of an intermediate type known as the hedgehog because in many ways that is what it looks like. It consists of a horizontal pot boiler and inserted in it are a number of short lengths of copper rod. The burner supplies heat not only to the boiler surface but also to the copper rods, which transfer the heat higher into the boiler contents than is achieved with the plain pot boiler.

The other half of the design is that of a normal type of horizontal boiler with a number of heat tubes going vertically through. The heat from the burner travels along the tubes and heats the water inside. It is a more efficient system than the hedgehog but has the disadvantage that there is heat travelling upwards along the whole length of the boiler and it is therefore necessary to make a cover that extends the length of the boiler. Although it involves additional work leaving the top open is not a

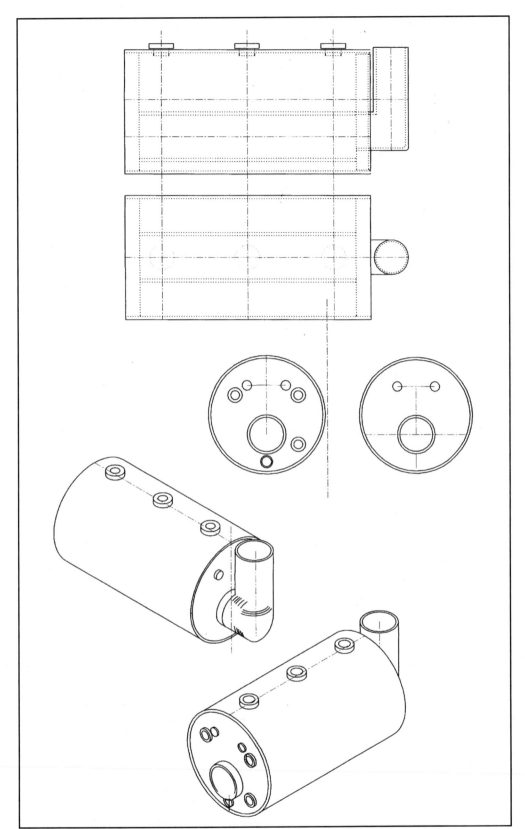

This centre flue type boiler is very popular. The drawing shows details of the boiler shell with isometric views to aid construction.

very practical proposition as there is a distinct possibility of being burned if one leans across it to make adjustments to the engine. The usual method of dealing with this problem is to make a suitable cover, rather like an inverted trough and to put a single flue into that, thus diverting the heat through the single tube rather than it coming from several.

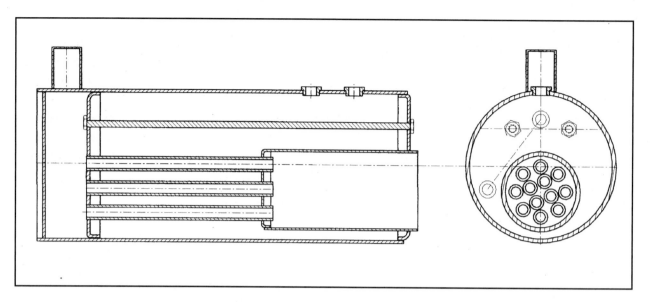

A smplified marine style boiler.

A simple yet efficient boiler made entirely from central heating tube.

Apart from the tubes the boiler is made in the same way as all the others, except that the one shown has the flange plates on the outside. Readers do not have to follow the idea but it is something which will suit some builders as there is less need for complete accuracy when making the flange plates.

The two internal spikes are made from copper rod and in the case of the boiler shown are silver soldered straight to the shcll; the alternative has already been mentioned. The usual test plugs for water level are fitted and at the top is a bush for a small two-way turret, to contain the regulator and safety valve, the latter doubling as a filler plug.

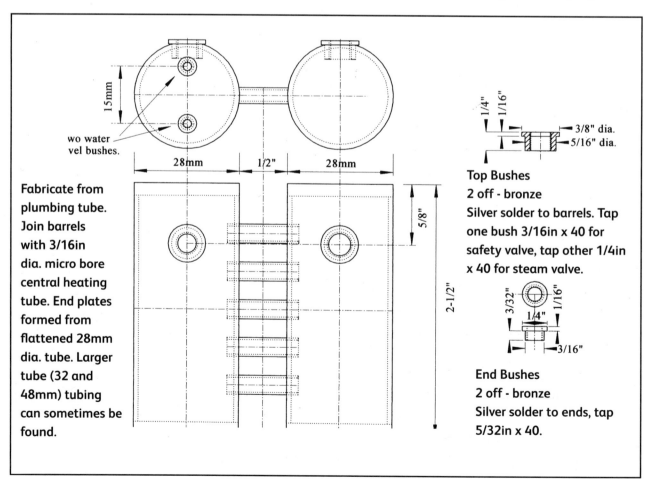

15mm

wo water vel bushes.

28mm   1/2"   28mm

5/8"

2-1/2"

Fabricate from plumbing tube. Join barrels with 3/16in dia. micro bore central heating tube. End plates formed from flattened 28mm dia. tube. Larger tube (32 and 48mm) tubing can sometimes be found.

1/4" 1/16" →3/8" dia. →5/16" dia.

Top Bushes
2 off - bronze
Silver solder to barrels. Tap one bush 3/16in x 40 for safety valve, tap other 1/4in x 40 for steam valve.

3/32" 1/16" 1/4" →3/16"

End Bushes
2 off - bronze
Silver solder to ends, tap 5/32in x 40.

9
Boiler Fittings

Boiler fittings are the essential link between the boiler and engine, fortunately for most marine purposes very few are necessary but without them it will not be possible to operate. As the boiler will be connected to the engine via a length of pipe, perhaps dealing with that is a good point at which to start.

Nuts and olives

By far the most secure way to connect pipe work to the engine for any type of fitting is to solder the two together, preferably with silver solder, but if not soft solder can do the job quite well. Providing the joints are sound, there can be no leaks and no danger of things coming apart and the whole idea has a great deal to recommend it, if the situation is such that a solder joint will do, then that is the way it should be done. So why then do we need any other method of making connections? There are a couple of very good reasons: first of all it is quite likely that from time to time it will be necessary to dismantle things, if they are silver soldered, it will be impossible, if soft soldered, nearly impossible and in all probability impossible to assemble them again. Also many situations make soldering of any type virtually impossible, because of the amount of metal involved soldering irons will not do the job and the flame

from even the smallest blowlamp is likely to cause irreparable damage to other items nearby. Therefore most joints will have to be screwed together in one way or another.

There is no objection to screwing a pipe straight into an item, if it is possible to do so, in which case a fine thread should be used, however as a rule it is not practical to do so. Usually there just plainly is not room or a bend in the pipe makes doing so impractical.

Union nuts

Most pipe work will therefore be connected via a union nut, the olive,

A union nut and olive, there are two types of the latter, those with a sleeve as shown here and others that do not have tails. All olives, whatever the type should be silver soldered to the pipe.

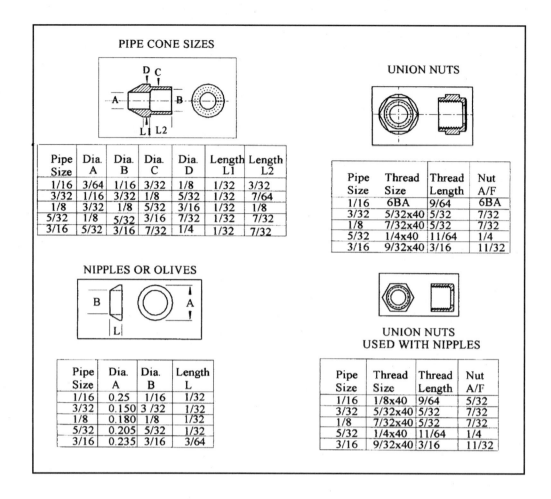

PIPE CONE SIZES

Pipe Size	Dia. A	Dia. B	Dia. C	Dia. D	Length L1	Length L2
1/16	3/64	1/16	3/32	1/8	1/32	3/32
3/32	1/16	3/32	1/8	5/32	1/32	7/64
1/8	3/32	1/8	5/32	3/16	1/32	1/8
5/32	1/8	5/32	3/16	7/32	1/32	7/32
3/16	5/32	3/16	7/32	1/4	1/32	7/32

UNION NUTS

Pipe Size	Thread Size	Thread Length	Nut A/F
1/16	6BA	9/64	6BA
3/32	5/32x40	5/32	7/32
1/8	7/32x40	5/32	7/32
5/32	1/4x40	11/64	1/4
3/16	9/32x40	3/16	11/32

NIPPLES OR OLIVES

Pipe Size	Dia. A	Dia. B	Length L
1/16	0.25	1/16	1/32
3/32	0.150	3/32	1/32
1/8	0.180	1/8	1/32
5/32	0.205	5/32	1/32
3/16	0.235	3/16	3/64

UNION NUTS
USED WITH NIPPLES

Pipe Size	Thread Size	Thread Length	Nut A/F
1/16	1/8x40	9/64	5/32
3/32	5/32x40	5/32	7/32
1/8	7/32x40	5/32	7/32
5/32	1/4x40	11/64	1/4
3/16	9/32x40	3/16	11/32

A selection of
piping fitted with
nuts and olives,
both types of
olives have been
used.

as it is so called making a suitable method of preventing the pipe from being released. So let us start with the nuts, which are a little different from the normal type of nuts used to secure parts together. The main difference is that they have a lip on the end that prevents the olive from pulling through.

This means that in order to make them, a piece of hexagon material is first drilled a close clearance size for the pipe that is to be used. It is then opened out for must of its length, to the size that is suitable for tapping the thread, but before it is tapped the end section that has not been opened has to be made flat, in order that pressure can be applied to the olive. The usual tool for doing this is known as a 'D' Bit and is most frequently home made. Anyone not wishing to go to the trouble of making one can either use a milling cutter, or grind the end off a suitable sized drill and make that flat.

Making 'D' bits

It is not difficult to make 'D' bits; all that is required is a short length of the correct sized silver steel. The end of that is filed to half its diameter (and that means exactly half), the steel then has to be hardened and tempered, although if one is only proposing to make three or four nuts the latter operation can be dispensed with.

To harden the steel it must be heated until it turns the colour of a boiled carrot and then quenched in water. In theory it should be quenched in whale oil, but that is hardly practical these days and if it is decided to use oil it must be a vegetable one, like rape seed oil. Oil does not improve the hardening in any way but it is possible for the steel to crack when dropped into cold water, something that is most unlikely to happen with such a small component. Once the steel has cooled it has to be cleaned to its original bright state, in order to temper it, as it turns black when quenched. Cleaning can be done with emery paper, but it is a 'dickens of a job' and a lot of effort can be avoided if before it is heated, it is covered in washing up liquid, for some reason this prevents too much discolouration.

Tempering is carried out because with the steel in its very hard state it soon chips, and the cutting edge in particular will become ragged and blunt. As stated above, this is unlikely if the tool is to be used a strictly limited number of times. To draw the temper as it is called, the tool must be heated again until the oxide that forms on the surface at the cutting edge becomes a dark straw colour and it is then again quenched. When steel is heated the oxide colour starts to change, it does not stop when the heat source is removed, the colour continues changing, which is something we do not want because if not very careful the colour will go beyond the dark straw to blue and it will not then suit the purpose. There are a number of ways of preventing this from happening; one is to get a small tray of sand and lay the job on top of it, then heat the sand from below, the colour of the steel will change very slowly and in a controlled manner, not suddenly flashing from one to the other and the tool can be quenched at exactly the right moment. The other is to apply the flame to the end that does not have a cutting edge and

watch the colour change, it will spread along the tool, when the cutting end is right quench it quickly. It will be necessary to be quite quick, as the colour will move much more rapidly along the thinner section of metal and it will probably be necessary to move the tool towards the water a second or so prior to the colour reaching the end. It can also be tempered by laying it on an electric hot plate, an idea that works in exactly the same way as the bed of sand.

Once the tool has been tempered the cutting edge can be sharpened, either with an oilstone or with a diamond lap. It should not be necessary to grind the edge, as long as sufficient care has been taken when filing the original shape.

Having acquired the necessary tool it can be used to flatten the inside of the nut, a job that should be done on the lathe, the nut can then be tapped. It might be necessary to grind the end of a tap flat in order to run the thread right along the nut. Even plug taps are not always as square ended as they might be and if left in the original condition may not go right to the end of the nut.

Olives

The most common way of joining fittings is to put a thread in the fitting and make an olive with a matching taper, a system that has stood the test of time. Making the olive is simple enough; take a length of brass or bronze of the exact diameter of the inside of the thread area of the nut, then drill it to the diameter of the pipe it is to be fitted to. Machine the end to the required taper and part off.

The tapered olive system works very well, providing that the tapers are a reasonable match, if not leaks are likely to occur. For anyone with limited experience in using a lathe there is a better way and that is to ensure the end of the fitting is absolutely flat, something that as a rule can be achieved by simply facing across. Then, instead of making tapered olives make small thick washers and solder those to the pipe. The pressure of the nut will bring both surfaces into contact and when the nut is tightened the pressure will force the two

Commercially made safety valves of varying types, the one on the left is useful where headroom is limited as the release spring is inside the boiler.

flat surfaces against each other. If you still do not have the confidence that a sound joint will result, make the nut slightly longer than required and fit an 'O' ring between the two surfaces.

Regulators

Unlike the locomotive or traction engine a model boat does not require a very sophisticated regulator, and in fact some form of on - off tap that allows a little adjustment to the steam flow, is all that is needed. If the boat is to be radio-controlled, a fairly long lever to control it will do the job nicely and fitting a regulator with fine adjustment is an absolute waste of time. A similar device can be used for non radio-controlled boats, or alternatively for those a screw down valve will do. The important thing with either device is that it can be shut down completely and will not leak steam.

Safety valves

All boilers should be fitted with an efficient safety valve that is set to discharge at the maximum working pressure of the boiler. It must be capable of preventing the pressure in the boiler from rising by more than 10% above working pressure. The valve should be regularly examined and tested to ensure that it is in good working order. For maximum safety a boiler should be fitted with two safety valves, one set to discharge at a very slightly higher pressure than the other. However while two valves are the perfect answer, realistically in most case, because model marine boilers are so small, a single valve only will be used.

It is highly unlikely that anything other than a standard type of valve will be required and while in full size there were a number of differing designs, most have no value in model marine work. Where there is limited headroom

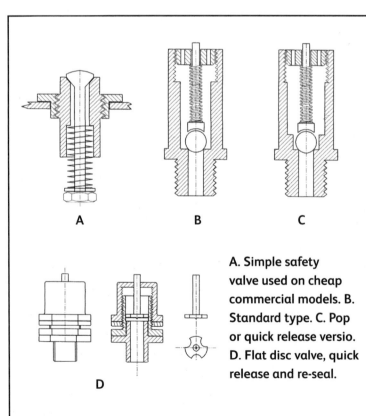

A. Simple safety valve used on cheap commercial models. B. Standard type. C. Pop or quick release versio. D. Flat disc valve, quick release and re-seal.

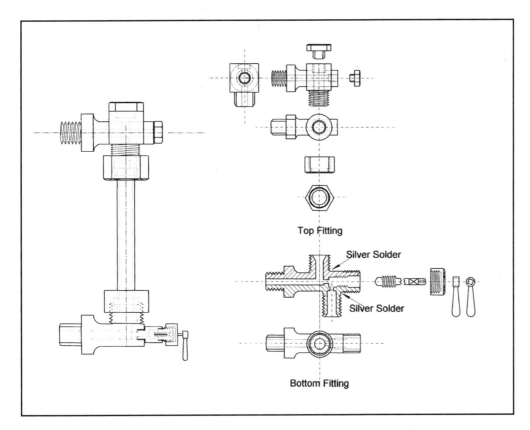

Top Fitting

Silver Solder

Silver Solder

Bottom Fitting

Common type
of water gauge;
on the left is a
completed gauge,
on the right the
necessary parts.

it might be preferable to fit the type of valve that fits inside the boiler, otherwise the type that is fitted outside is best. By changing the shape of the valve seating arrangement it is possible to produce a valve that will release with a loud popping sound, there is an advantage with this type of valve in that they generally release much faster than the more usual arrangement. The latter will often simmer, giving a small discharge before releasing the pressure in full. It is largely a matter of personal choice as to which type is chosen.

Making ones own safety valve is quite easy and has the advantage that it can be made to a design suitable for the boiler on which it is to be used. The springs should be of stainless steel or bronze and can be wound on a lathe, however for anyone who does not wish to make their own, a good source of supply is the return spring from ball point pens of the type where the writing tip clicks in and out. They are stainless steel and as

a rule are capable of being compressed to a point where they will be nicely adjustable for pressures between 20 – 60 p.s.i. If a ball is to be used for the valve, the seating must be flat, which is another job for the 'D' Bit. Other types of valve should be ground in, by rotating them backwards and forwards in the seat, using a mild grinding paste such as a brass cleaner, or toothpaste.

Water gauges

Although a water gauge is desirable, it depends on the type of steam plant as to whether or not it is necessary. Simple plants that have been designed in such a way that they work on a single filling of water so that the burner will go out either at the same time or slightly before the water runs out, do not need to have a water gauge fitted, there is really no point in doing so. Two screw in plugs, with water passages are used and the boiler is filled so that water is just running from the top one, the lower

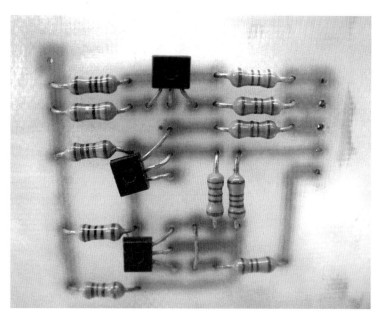

The electronic Water Gauge designed by Roy Amsbury.

one simply being there as a means of making a double check. If it is undone, then as long as water seeps from it, there is sufficient water in the boiler. If steam emerges instead of water, it is time to shut off the heat as the water level is low, but the boiler has not actually run dry. If the top one is opened with the burner working, steam should in that case emerge. Because the boiler is not going to be replenished it does not matter what the water level is in between times. It is though essential that the burner is adjusted so that it will burn for no longer than it takes for the water to drop to the level of the lower plug. Generally it will be a case of working to get this right by trial and error.

While the above system is perfectly sound it must be admitted that it is always a comfort to know the level of the water in the boiler. The same two bushes used to accommodate the plugs mentioned above, can be used to fit a water gauge, Water gauges are not difficult to make and they can be purchased if one wishes. It is important to ensure that if a gauge is fitted then the level of the water is easy to see. This is not always the case with plain glass tubing

and special tubing that has a blue or red line along its length is recommended. The alternative, which probably works better still, is to make a back plate and paint diagonal white and blue stripes on it, In both cases the level of the water creates an uneven level line, making it obvious what the level is.

Fitting the glass tube in such a way that it does not break can be difficult until one gets the hang of things. When it is hot, the slightest knock will cause the glass to shatter unless it is properly fitted. At one time protection was provided by the use of graphited string wrapped around the glass at each end. This has now been superseded with the use of 'O' rings that are either fitted around the outside of the glass or in many cases they rest on each end of it.

A blow down arrangement must be provided at the bottom of the fitting, unfortunately water does not just find a nice level, because of the air and turbulence inside the boiler bubbles frequently appear in the glass, giving a false reading. By opening the blow down cock, a small jet of water is allowed out, taking the air bubble with it. Of course if the boat is in the middle of a lake it is not possible to clear the glass in this way, but at least the blow down valve will ensure that the amount of water in the boiler is known before the vessel leaves the bank.

Sometimes a shut down valve is fitted at the top of the gauge to allow the water or steam to be cut off, should the glass break. The effect of this happening is for a cloud of steam to be ejected, which in nearly every instance will make it impossible to get at the valve to close it and by the time it has been reached, the boiler will have run dry anyway. Therefore fitting such a valve is of doubtful value and will only be useful with a very large boiler.

If the gauge glass should break and the contents of the boiler be evacuated unexpectedly there is no need to panic. Keep hands, etc. away from the hot steam and at the first opportunity remove the heat source. There is no danger of this causing a boiler to burst, as all the pressure will escape through the gaps left by the glass breaking. It may very well get extremely hot if it is not possible to remove the heat immediately, but providing the boiler is soundly made it will come to no harm. There is likely to be enough heat however to melt any soft solder that might have been used on piping, etc.

Some years ago the late Roy Amsbury designed an electronic water gauge, consisting of two probes that were fitted in the boiler, connected via a circuit to a pair of light emitting diodes. A green light showed if the water level was satisfactory and a red one when water was getting a bit short. It was a clever device and had the advantage that the level indicators could be situated away from the boiler if one so wished.

Pressure gauges

Once again, with a very simple boiler and burner arrangement, fitting a pressure gauge is not a necessity. The safety valve or valves can be set to discharge at the desired pressure and as long as the boiler and burner are adjusted in such a way that there will be no great excess of steam, the safety valve will take care of the pressure situation. It is usual to use a pressure gauge as a guide as to when to start the engine and if one is not fitted, it can be started as soon as the safety valve blows off.

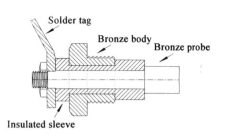

The probes consist of a bronze body threaded to fit the bushes in the boiler - an insulated sleeve that fits inside the body and a bronze probe or electrode that fits inside the sleeve. The sleeve and probe are secured with a nut that also secures a solder tag.

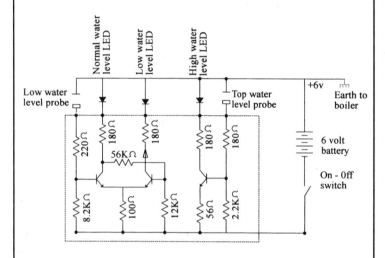

Transistors - Ferranti ZTX302 or equivelant.
Items shown in dotted box are on the printed circuit board.

If it is decided to use a pressure gauge there is no reason why it should not be home made, although it is something that is rarely done and usually a

Roy Amesbury design theoretical circuit. The lower level LED could be replaced with a relay to drive an electrical water pump.

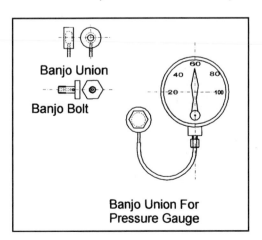

Banjo Union For Pressure Gauge

Banjo union for pressure gauge fitting.

commercially made item will be used. The gauge should be capable of reading at least 20% above the working pressure, which should be clearly marked on the face of the gauge, preferably in red. In theory the gauge should be as large as possible as the larger it is, the easier it is to see the reading and also a large gauge is more likely to be accurate than a smaller one. Fitting a large gauge may impair the appearance of the boat and therefore it must be left to the individual to decide the appropriate size.

Pressure gauges should always be mounted via a 'U' tube, or siphon, which as the name suggests is a thin 'U' shaped tube. This has the effect of absorbing any rapid rises in pressure and thus protecting the gauge from damage.

Non-return valves

If a pump of any sort is fitted then it is going to be necessary to fit a non-return valve, to prevent, water and steam from flowing back to the source of supply. Such valves are very easy to make but again can be purchased if one so wishes. All fittings should be made of bronze rather than brass, and this is particularly the case with non return valves that seem to suffer more from the effects of de-zincification than other fittings.

Turrets

The steam turret is a device that allows two or more accessories to be connected to a single point of outlet. Using one would allow say a safety valve and regulator to be fitted to the same boiler bush, which can be an advantage as it ensures everything is adjacent. Because a turret is designed for a particular situation it is almost inevitable that it will need to be specially made. It is not a difficult task, requiring only a short length of hollow section material with

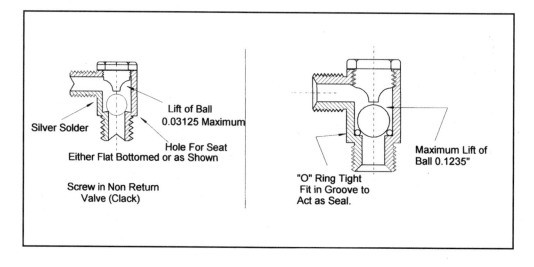

Silver Solder

Lift of Ball
0.03125 Maximum

Hole For Seat
Either Flat Bottomed or as Shown

Screw in Non Return
Valve (Clack)

Maximum Lift of
Ball 0.1235"

"O" Ring Tight
Fit in Groove to
Act as Seal.

a screw fitting, that will allow it to be connected to the boiler and a couple or so screw fittings for the outlet. It should be kept to as neat proportions as possible as oversized turrets can easily spoil the appearance of any steam plants.

Whistles

Fitting a whistle is certainly not a necessity but it is something many people like to do and if one is used then the turret is a good idea, otherwise an extra outlet from the boiler will be needed. Actually making the whistle is not at all difficult, but getting it to sound right is another matter altogether. The high-pitched note that is the familiar sound of a steam launch approaching

can be reproduced reasonably easily; the low throaty growl of the larger vessels is more difficult. Whistles are easy to make but only trial and error can enable one to produce the required note.

A small turret giving two outlets and some examples of home made check valves.

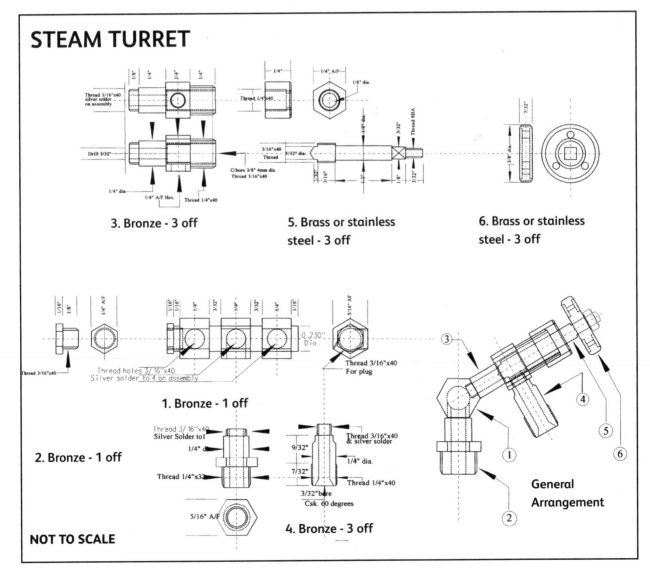

STEAM TURRET

3. Bronze - 3 off

5. Brass or stainless steel - 3 off

6. Brass or stainless steel - 3 off

1. Bronze - 1 off

2. Bronze - 1 off

4. Bronze - 3 off

General Arrangement

NOT TO SCALE

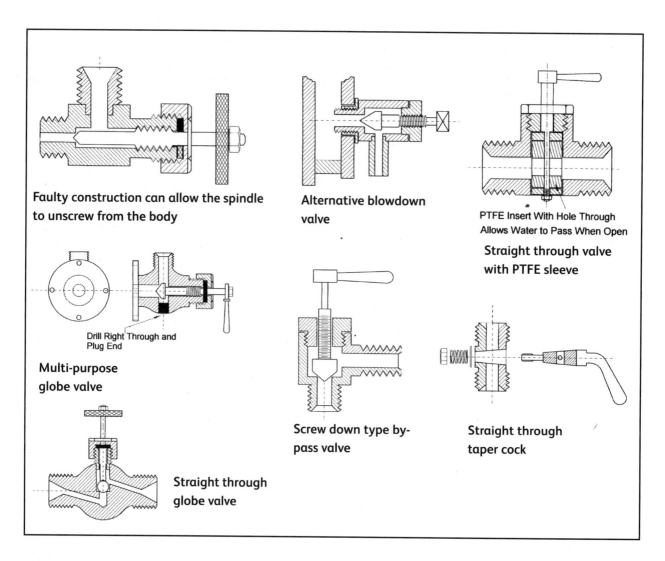

Faulty construction can allow the spindle to unscrew from the body

Alternative blowdown valve

PTFE Insert With Hole Through Allows Water to Pass When Open

Straight through valve with PTFE sleeve

Drill Right Through and Plug End

Multi-purpose globe valve

Screw down type by-pass valve

Straight through taper cock

Straight through globe valve

Unless one is prepared to be satisfied with a sound that is little more than a squeak, any whistle is going to be vastly out of proportion to the boat and therefore requires hiding away somewhere. As when it is sounded steam will be emitted, care should be taken to situate it somewhere that the condensation caused will have no effect on the working of the boat. When a full sized ship sounds its horn or whistle a wisp of steam appears from it and as a rule it will be situated on the funnel. A nice finishing touch is to fit a tiny dummy instrument and run a length of very thin tubing to it. The tubing is connected to the steam pipe that operates the whistle and hey presto every time the whistle sounds, a wisp of steam appears.

Securing fittings

Nearly all fittings on model boilers are constructed so that they screw into boiler bushes. In full sized practice this is not the way they fitted at all, they invariably were bolted to a flange with three bolts, or perhaps more likely three studs fitted with nuts. Occasionally on smaller items it may have been just two studs, while on very large ones such as a regulator, there would have been a whole ring of studs and nuts. They would be spaced at one and half or twice the across flat size of the nuts.

Modellers seeking to obtain scale appearance will do well to make their fittings in the same way as nothing looks less like the real thing than fittings screwed into a hefty bush. In small scale, securing fittings in that manner, although desirable, can be to say the least, tedious work. It is possible to get the best of both worlds, by putting dummy studs and nuts on the flange of a fitting that screws in. Drill clearance sized holes and then simply slip in the stud with the nut fitted, and hold the whole assembly secure with a retaining compound. Once assembled only you will know the true story.

10
Firing Methods

When building or running a steamboat a means of heating water to generate the steam is a necessity, so before dwelling on types of burners to use for this purpose, let us start with a look at the possible dangers involved.

Firstly there is always the possibility of burning or scalding oneself, and care must be taken to ensure that hands or any other part of the body do not come into contact with hot surfaces or steam. It is a matter of common sense, which the owner of the boat will be well aware of, but interested bystanders might not, so it is also necessary to ensure that other people do not burn or scald themselves either.

Whatever method is used to fire a boiler there are a number of dangers involved, for example methylated spirits burns with an almost invisible flame, that is not easily detected, particularly on a hot sunny day and therefore can cause nasty burns, when one is not aware that the fuel is alight.

We rarely, if ever, see paraffin burners nowadays, in fact their use is not even discussed in this book, but it might be possible if a used boat was bought that it used that type of burner. The danger is that the fuel burns under pressure, and also that the outlet needs pre-heating, the latter is generally done

with methylated spirits, which as we see above burns with a near invisible flame. It is very easy to believe that the pre-heating fuel has burned away and to pressurise the paraffin at a temperature below that at which it vaporises. The result of this is to shoot a long length of burning paraffin over a considerable distance. If we realise that flame-throwers used by the armed forces in World War Two, worked on this principle, the danger becomes more obvious. Oil fired boilers work on a similar system and the same danger is present when they are used.

Liquid Petroleum Gas or LPG as it is better known is now a very popular fuel and several varieties are sold, the dangers associated with all are similar. Firstly the gas as described is in a liquid form and is stored under pressure. Different gases are stored at different pressures and in the case of Propane in particular this is very high. We therefore have three danger areas: an inadequate pressure vessel to hold the fuel that could result in an explosion. The possibility of the gas spilling as a liquid in which case it can remain undetected in the well of a boat, subsequently catching fire, as well as the possibility of fire when it is in the gaseous state. Finally, very occasionally we may come across a boat that has coal firing. At one time these were very popular but nowadays very rarely seen and there is then the danger of hot coal falling on a combustible material.

All the above facts should not be allowed to prevent anyone enjoying the pleasure of running a model steamboat; thousands do so every year without mishap, so go ahead and enjoy the pleasure of steam but take care.

Satisfactorily firing a boiler is not as straightforward as connecting a battery to an electric motor. Of course a unit that has been purchased is, or at least should be quite efficient, but a home made one can be a little unpredictable. Especially if the builder has not dabbled in this sort of thing before and to get the best results will almost inevitably mean some experimenting. There are many factors to be taken into account; the size of the boiler and the thickness of the shell are probably the first to be considered. If a boiler shell is too thick, a large amount of the heat from the burner will be used in heating the shell, rather than the water it contains, this does not mean reducing the thickness of the shell to unsafe proportions but at the same time do not use metal of a heavier gauge than needed when it is not necessary to do so. Boilers described herein have a safety factor of at least ten.

Fuels

The type of fuel to be used is the next obvious thing to consider and there are several from which to select. Coal firing, which was the method used for many years in full size is possible but difficult. Although there is nothing quite like the smell associated with a steam engine running from a coal fired boiler, it is not a fuel that can really be recommended, but no doubt some dedicated enthusiasts might wish to give it a try. Once the fire is alight and burning, control of it from the bank of a pond is almost impossible and the fire can only be attended to from the bank. Unlike the more popular fuels it is also impossible to gauge the length of time the fire will be burning.

Add to that the danger involved should hot coal or embers overspill on to any wooden structure in the boat and it really does seem that coal firing should remain a pleasant dream.

Oil firing

The use of oil for firing boilers was wide spread, once suitable methods of vaporising the oil had been devised. It is used extensively in full size, though it is not really very adaptable for use in model boilers and has no place in the modern hobby as it is of doubtful use in a model boat. It involves using a heavy fuel oil and vaporising it with the use of a pre-heater and then injecting it into the fire as a fine mist, the complications when the system is miniaturised are considerable. Many years ago the use of paraffin was quite popular, it was burned using a similar system to oil firing. This vaporised the paraffin, which burned with a good hot flame. Readers who can recall the old type of paraffin blowlamp and Primus cooking stoves will know the system. It has long been superseded by more modern methods. It was not an easy one to use and there was a danger that if the jets did not get hot enough the paraffin burned without vaporising, in which case it would spill into the boat. Nevertheless many people preferred the use of paraffin to methylated spirits as it gave a considerably hotter flame.

Fuel tablets

If the boat is to be operated by a child then there is little doubt that in the interests of safety fuel tablets are the best answer. They are a long way from being the most efficient and in addition to lacking in heat output, discharge thick black oily soot on the underside of the boiler that, unless cleaned off from time to time, actually absorbs the heat generated by the tablets. In spite of these drawbacks, the tablets are the safest type of fuel by far, they burn for a short period and there is nothing to spill. Many people find them difficult to use. The main reason for this is that a good quantity of air is required to get good combustion and all too frequently the tray in which they are burned limits the amount of air available.

Methylated spirits

For many years a favourite with those that like to run model steam engines, methylated spirits is still a very popular fuel. There are probably two reasons for this: firstly the fact that making a receptacle in which to use it is much easier than making one for use with LPG. Secondly it is far less dangerous, if LPG leaks it will seep into tiny spaces and ignite very quickly, which means it can cause quite a fire. Methylated spirits that gets away in the same fashion will rapidly evaporate, if it has not had the opportunity to do so and catches fire, that fire is localised and it is unlikely that anything other than the spilled spirit will be burned. At one time street entertainers in markets in London would spread methylated spirits on their hands and arms and set fire to it. There were no obvious signs of burning to the skin afterwards, showing how localised the flames are. It was not quite as straightforward as it seems, as prior to their act they coated their arms with soft soap, which acted as a barrier to the heat. *Readers should most definitely not try to emulate the trick as even though the flame is localised it can still cause serious burns.*

The spirit is easy to obtain and almost invariably will be coloured mauve or pink. The colour (methyl purple) has been added to a colourless liquid (ethyl alcohol) and is done for two reasons, firstly it makes the spirit more visible and so easier to handle, secondly it also alters the taste, which is intended to stop people from drinking it. The quality of the spirit varies considerably, for example if it is bought from a DIY store it seems to lack heat when burned, bought from a chemist it is usually a little better and will give more heat. If it is purchased at a good quality tool store, as a rule it will have a higher calorific value, particularly when bought in a reasonable quantity, rather than a small bottle. Where it is bought therefore can make quite a difference to how the boat will operate and once a good source of supply has been found it is best to use that all the time.

Burners for methylated spirits will generally consist of a holding tank with an extension, frequently in the form of a tube, with one or more vertical tubes that hold wicks. The wicks serve to draw the spirit up from the reservoir and evaporate it. A complete flame has a good bluish colour and if it is any other colour the air is not being properly burned. As with all fuels a quantity of air is necessary to supply the oxygen the flame requires. A common problem is to place the flame too close to the boiler, which will result in inefficiency.

The level of the fuel in the tank generally should be below the level of the top of the wicks; otherwise the fuel will spill through the jets and catch fire outside the burner. This can be very limiting on the amount of fuel in use and so many people fit a needle valve to limit the amount of fuel released to the wicks and thus prevent it from escaping. Adjustment of the needle is a case of trial and error. A more advanced method of air control is to use what is generally termed a chicken feed. In this case an additional pipe is introduced and air pressure controls the amount of fuel released to the wicks at any one time. It is quite a good system and can give an extended run to an engine.

The efficiency of a methylated spirit burner can be considerably improved by the addition of air ducts that attract fuel towards the flame. Preheating it in the process, this vaporises the spirit increasing the amount of heat generated. The easiest way of making these air ducts is to just simply drill a row of holes round the base of the wick tubes.

Other methods of increasing the amount of heat generated are to use a sheet of ceramic material or nichrome wire, (this is the wire that used to be used in radiant type electric fires and the elements in most fan heaters), that fits over the flame. The ceramic sheet is the material used to increase the heat generated by a gas fire, it should have a series of tiny holes drilled in it to aid combustion, the use of both of these materials is also relevant to firing with LPG and will be dealt with at greater length later.

Liquid Petroleum Gas

Liquid petroleum Gas or LPG as it is better known comes in several forms although usually only Butane and Propane or a mixture of the two are used domestically, **Beware these gases are very dangerous and must be treated with respect**. They are much heavier than air and collect in an invisible explosive pool at the bottom of a boat if containers or fittings are allowed to leak. **All experiments and tests must be made in the open air out of doors.**

Liquefied petroleum gas also called liquid petroleum gas, LPG, LP gas, or autogas) is a mixture of hydrocarbon gases. A "stenching" agent is added so that leaks can be detected easily by smell. LPG is manufactured during the refining of crude oil, or extracted from oil or gas streams as they emerge from the ground, it was first produced in 1910 by Dr. Walter Snelling, and the first commercial products appeared in 1912.

At normal temperatures and pressures, LPG will evaporate. Because of this, it is supplied in pressurised steel bottles. In order to allow for thermal expansion of the contained liquid, these bottles should not be filled completely; typically, they are filled to between 80% and 85% of their capacity. The ratio between the volumes of the vaporised gas and the liquefied gas varies depending on composition, pressure and temperature, but is typically around 250:1. The pressure at which LPG becomes liquid, called its vapour pressure, likewise varies depending on composition and temperature; for example, it is approximately 33 p.s.i. (2.2 bar) for pure Butane at 20°C, and approximately 325 p.s.i. (22 bar) for pure Propane at 55°C. Propane therefore requires a stronger tank than Butane, and because of the higher pressure at which it is stored it is more difficult to control when used in very small burners. These figures are approximate and there will anyway be a slight variation in pressure depending on the ambient temperature.

It follows that for use in a boat, the gas must be stored in a suitable container capable of withstanding the necessary pressure. As all pressure vessels should initially be tested to twice working pressure the Propane container must be able to withstand pressures up to 650p.s.i. or 44 bar. Using thick walled tubing there is no reason why such a container cannot be made in the home workshop. However it is most unlikely that a club boiler inspector would have facilities to test the container to such a pressure and most societies will want to ensure that a gas container is properly tested.

In addition to plain Butane or Propane, fuels are frequently supplied as a mixture of each, varying from Butane/Propane at a ratio of 90/10 in stages to Butane/Propane at a mix of 60/40. It is therefore beholden on anyone building a container for LPG to check what gas or mixture it is proposed to use and to make the tank of sufficient strength to suit. The Model Power Boat Association has a code of practice to be followed and has specified the pressures at which tanks should be tested and local Model Boat Societies will almost certainly have the same requirements, or will use their own standards. If it is proposed to use a boat at an event organised by a local society or the Model Power Boat Association, then a suitable test certificate for both boiler and gas tank will be required.

There is nothing to prevent anyone using a boat that does not have a certificate if it is not an event organised by a club or association. However it would be most foolhardy not to test the tank, to ensure it is absolutely safe. The testing procedure for a tank is the same as that described for boilers. Whilst a leak may be acceptable with a boiler this is most certainly not the case with a gas tank, when any leak will pose a very real danger to anyone in the near vicinity.

The lower pressure at which Butane is stored means a test at 66p.s.i. or 4.4 bar and it should be well within the capabilities of a club boiler inspector, in addition the lower pressure means a more manageable flame and so Butane has quite a few advantages as a fuel as far as safety is concerned. The difficulty involved in getting gas tanks tested has caused many modellers a bit of a headache, so some use a small cylinder that can be purchased for use with camping stoves. Although these containers are indeed small and flat they are still only suitable for a comparatively large boat, even so they are a most convenient way of storing fuel and making a valve to regulate the discharge of the fuel is comparatively easy. The release valve should always be situated at the highest point on a tank. Remember the fuel is stored in liquid form and a release valve low down would result in the gas being released in that form instead of as a vapour and it would be highly dangerous.

Some vessels are simply just not large enough to be able to use the camping stove type of container and this will mean either buying or making a suitable tank. Many home made ones are designed to be filled from a commercial tank, similar to the one referred to above, but larger and fitted with a screw connection, by connecting the two and literally pouring the liquid gas from one to the other. With well-made valves the idea can be successful and does not appear to be frowned upon by some societies. In spite of that it is not proposed to give details of the equipment needed, because there is a very real danger, unless the conversion equipment is made to a suitably high standard.

Commercially made refillable tanks are filled via a valve that mates with a nozzle from an LPG gas tank, designed for transferring fuel into cigarette lighters and the valves can be purchased. If one is fitted to a tank then do not forget that the gas is in its liquid state and must therefore be allowed to fall into the new receptacle. It is surprising how many people do not consider this fact when building tanks, with the result that it is difficult to get a full complement of gas in.

Although not immediately obvious there is another advantage to the use of LPG that is the fact that the height of the boiler can be considerably reduced as the burner can be very narrow. A well designed gas burner with adequate air supply will generally have a lower flame height than is obtainable with methylated spirits.

Another alternative for the use of LPG is to use one of the small pencil type blowlamps that are available, these can be quite effective in a centre flue boiler, with the flame directed along the flue. The flue should contain a couple of coils of nichrome wire which will then give a good radiant heat.

For those wishing to make their own gas tanks solid drawn brass tube should be used, it should be of a thickness of about 15% of the diameter. The ends should be made from brass sheet, or slices from a brass bar approximately 50% thicker than the tube walls. They should be recessed into the tubing with a lip and silver soldered in place. Sizes over one inch diameter should have a stay to support the ends; a maximum diameter of two inches is recommended. Both the filler valve and take-off connection to be fitted at the highest point, using brass bushes, silver soldered in place.

Making burners - fuel tablets

Very little is required to make a burner for use with fuel tablets. A simple tray folded up from a piece of mild steel, with some form of handle so that the tablets can be lit and then slid in position, is all that is required. One thing that should be watched out for is that the sides of the tray are not made too high. Doing so will restrict the flow of air and the tablets will not give off a true heat. If it is thought that making a small lip will pose a danger should the burner be used by a young person, then a series of holes round the sides will put matters right. As with all flames the flow of air that gives the flame oxygen is most important and must not be restricted in any way.

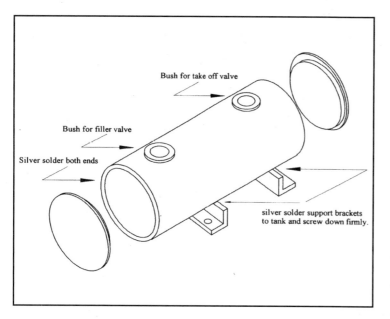

Bush for take off valve

Bush for filler valve

Silver solder both ends

silver solder support brackets
to tank and screw down firmly.

LPG tank fabrication - ends are best machined from solid with a lip fitting. All joints should be silver soldered.

Methylated spirits

Over the years literally hundreds of designs for spirit burners have been published, some have been more successful than others and again the reason for the least successful ones has been the fact that insufficient air could be drawn into the flame. The shape of the burner will of course depend on the type of boiler; a vertical one requiring a round burner a horizontal one a rectangular shape.

Round burners can be fabricated from a piece of tubing, or if one is lucky enough to find one a commercially made tin can be used. One or more tubes inserted in the top and allowed to stand a little proud will ensure the spirit does not flow out as it heats up. A similar arrangement can be made with a square tin for a horizontal boiler. The burner should be filled with an absorbent material, which should also protrude slightly through the tubes at the top, to form wicks. Long wicks have little advantage over shorter ones, they require the boiler to be set higher in order to have sufficient air to burn properly. At one time asbestos was a favourite for wicks but as it has now been established as a health hazard, other materials have to be used. It is possible to purchase wicks that are sold for lanterns and these can be reshaped to fit a burner. An alternative is lint of the sort used in first aid that can be bought at any chemist.

While the above arrangements are simple to make and work quite well, the amount of heat they supply is fairly limited and it is possible to make improvements. Quite a simple burner can be made using a tray like structure, filling it with the wick material and placing a piece of stainless steel gauze on the top. The gauze can be obtained by dismantling a strainer as used for preparation in cooking. A more recent innovation has been the use of a thin strip of ceramic material

Burners for methelated spirits, note the tops of the burner tubes should be at least level with the height of the fuel and if possible higher.

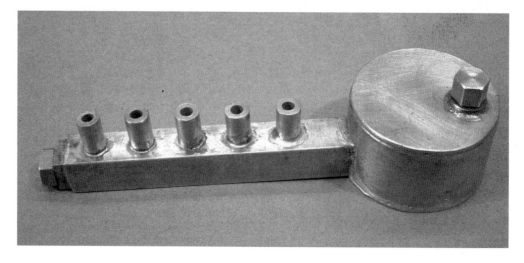

with numerous holes to allow the flames through, the wick material lying underneath the ceramic. This is obtainable from some suppliers of gas burners and is also stocked by some model shops.

The fact that the supply of spirit should be kept below the level of the burners has already been referred to. Therefore to increase the amount of time for which the burner will work, it is often desirable to have a spirit tank away from the actual burner and this can be connected via a narrow copper pipe, silver soldered to both tank and burner. Unless a valve is fitted the pipe must come from the top of the tank, otherwise the spirit will overflow and catch fire. Taking the pipe from near the top of the tank works reasonably well but improvements can be made by connecting it lower down and fitting a needle valve to control the flow, the spirit being allowed to dribble along to the burner. An even better arrangement is to fit the system known as a chicken feed, not only does it give a longer burning time but it is also safer than just allowing spirit to flow from a tank into the burner.

Remember that whatever type of burner is used, there must be sufficient clearance between the top of the burner and the bottom of the boiler to allow air to reach the flame and the flame should be in a position where the top spreads just a fraction. If the flame is flattened it will burn with a yellow colour and not give the required heat. It will also create soot, which will stick to the bottom of the boiler and create a heat barrier, so that it will gradually get less efficient.

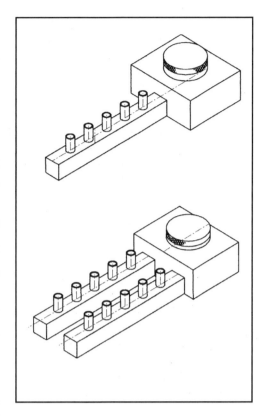

Two burners suitable for pot boiler firing Easy to fabricate from brass

LPG

Let us first of all consider how to make the burner and then decide on how the gas is to be stored and although this may sound like putting the cart before the horse it makes sense as the burner will be common to whatever type of storage system is decided upon.

There have been numerous descriptions of how to make burners, published in the model press, it is doubtful if many have surpassed the

Chicken hopper feed arrangement maintains the spirit level constant.

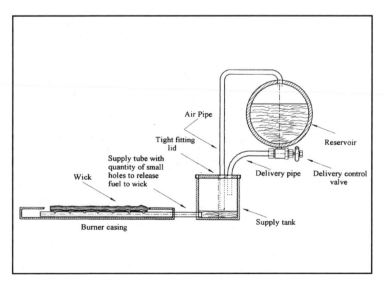

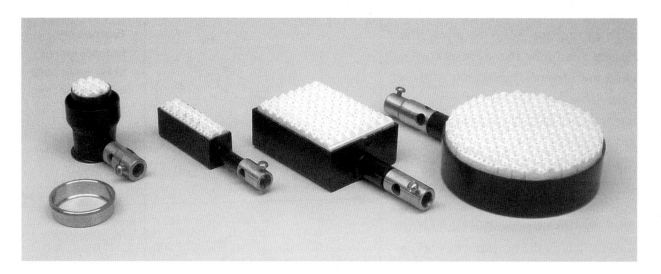

Commercially made gas burners, all are fitted with a layer of ceramic material to increase the heat output.

words of the late Don Gordon who did many experiments and spent may hours discussing the subject with interested parties at the Model Engineer Exhibition where he always had his own little corner to which numerous people would gravitate to listen to his advice. The following are Don's own words. These were written many years ago and number drills were quoted, these are now nearly obsolete and the equivalent metric size has been inserted, that apart his ideas are as relevant now as they were then:

"Broadly speaking there are two types of burner, the low flat type that goes under a boiler, and the other, rather like a torch that squirts a short jet of flame into a boiler that has fire tubes. The type of boiler with which it is to be used will therefore dictate the type of burner required. For both types there have been numerous designs published and the authors of the publications no doubt believe that their particular design is the best. Although it is easy to make and use a published design, it is a good idea to experiment with a number of variations of the design until one is found that really is the best for a particular purpose. There are so

many variables to contend with, such as sizes of jets, amount of air intake and controllability that it is well worthwhile trying a number of combinations until the best for your own individual use is found. Experimenting with many of the variables will be quite easy and will not involve a complete remake of the burner making it well worthwhile.

The low flat burner consists of a box, suitably shaped to fit under the boiler, air tubes pass through the box, and surrounding the top of each air tube is a ring of small holes, each of which will produce a tiny jet of flame. A mixing tube leads from the gas nipple to the burner box, ensuring a good supply of a suitable gas-air mix. Because part of the construction of the box area includes air tubes, this type of burner needs to be fitted so that there is space beneath it for the air to pass underneath and up through the tubes. Air is therefore induced into the mixture in two places, firstly near the gas jet close to the nipple through which the gas passes, in order that the two mix as they travel towards the position where they will be burned. Then there is what could be termed secondary air, which is induced through the air tubes.

The primary air, which is induced by

the gas jet near the nipple, mixes with the gas while travelling along a mixing tube into the burner box. Why do we need two types of air, why not just have a position somewhere that will allow as much air as can be induced from a single source? If you mix enough primary air with the gas to provide full combustion the mixture will be almost explosive, and will light back inside the burner instead of where we want it,. Not only could it create a fire inside the box, but also additionally it could cause an explosion, that would be immensely dangerous. By inducing more air at the point where combustion is required we ensure the flame is available in the correct place.

Good design is of course of the utmost importance, but equally, so is good workmanship, which is not to say that only a highly skilled engineer can make good burners, most people will be able to do so, providing they have the patience to take care. Also one must not be put off if something goes wrong and the

work has to be consigned to the scrap box. Everyone makes mistakes and when we look at those superb models at exhibitions it would be in many ways just as interesting to study the contents of the builder's scrap box. Of course we never get the opportunity to do so and so the assumption is that some very clever, highly skilled person has just got down and made the thing, which is not necessarily the case. Even the great Cherry Hill, (Now Cherry Hinds) who is generally acknowledged as the finest model engineer in the world, admits to not getting everything right first time, so don't worry if you can't.

One of the most important factors when making a burner is to ensure the nipple control needle is right and it must be said that in many ways this is the most difficult job of all, few if any lathes found in the home workshop will be suitable for machining the very thin taper, a spindle speed of several thousand revolutions a minute will be necessary to

A gas filling valve of the type that can be purchased. It is used with the type of gas cartridge supplied for cigarette lighters.

Parts salvaged from a cheap plastic cigarette lighter bought at a market stall. On the left is a gas filling valve and on the right a nipple that could be adapted for a burner. For good measure in the centre is a stainless steel spring that can be used for safety valves.

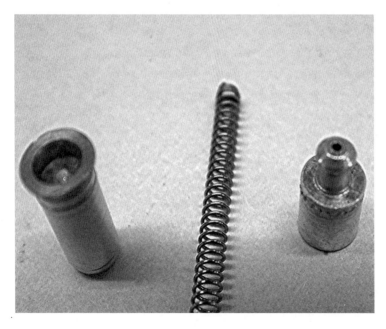

do the job properly. Also required will be a razor sharp tool, set exactly at centre height and either an extra fine feed to the saddle or a rock steady hand. This does not debar the average person from making the needle, but it may just be possible to avoid the necessity of doing so by using an ordinary needle as used for sewing. These do not have quite the right profile and different makes vary considerably in the shape of the point, but such needles have been used successfully and it could be worth a try. To do so will involve drilling a suitable piece of threaded material and sticking the needle in place with a retaining compound, it goes without saying that

the holding piece must be drilled very accurately.

Although the needle idea will work in some instances, it will not work every time and so one will have to be made and in view of the lathe requirements for turning, it will therefore be necessary to either use a file from the word go or partly machine it and then finish with a file. Filing work that is rotating is not of course generally recommended on grounds of safety and therefore not only must a chuck guard be in place but also great care must be taken when doing the job. Good support underneath the metal while the filing operations take place is essential and a wooden block works fine. It doesn't even have to be hard wood, as the material will partially embed itself into the block, giving even extra support. The file used to make the needle is of the utmost importance, although something of a start could be made with an ordinary fine file, to finish the job a number four cut precision file will be required and as long as the file has not previously been misused a nice fine finish will be the result.

Unfortunately this is not the end of the story as the needle requires a little more and in fact should be polished to a very high standard. This can be carried out with a metal polish or better still diamantine paste if you can get it. Even here there are numerous grades and the final polishing of the needle should be done with the finest available. The importance of the finish on the needle cannot be over-stressed. The length of the taper must be at least a quarter of an inch or 6mm and the best material to use for the needle is stainless steel.

Now for a few "design factors" or, rather, lessons learned from filling my scrap box with duff burners. The first lesson was that the nipple control needle has to have a very highly finished taper. Careful burnishing with diamantine to a brilliant polished surface seems to be essential to success. Examine it with a watchmaker's eyeglass and make sure that it is not bent at the extreme tip. The taper should be at least 1/4in long from the 10 BA core size to the point.

The second point is not so obvious: it applies critically to the box type burner.' What we are trying to do is to inject a tiny quantity of fuel, mixed with a large quantity of air, into a box whose only outlet is a lot of little holes. The mixture should emerge from the little holes just quickly enough to match the flame speed. If it comes out too fast the flames will be lifted off the burner and blow themselves out. If the mixture is too slow the flames will tend to burn back - light back - into the -burner box and try to melt it. More important, if the combined area of all the little holes is too small, pressure will build up inside the box and this will restrict the induction of primary air. It will not affect the injection of fuel as this is forced in by the gas pressure in the tank, so, with the same fuel but less air, the mixture will be too rich and will burn with a smoky yellow flame.

It is important, therefore, that the total outlet area of all the little holes in the burner is at least equal to the inlet area - that is, the area of the mixing tube. In practice, because of all the losses due to friction and other factors in the mixture for a successful burner has a mixing tube of 1/8in bore with a burner box having seven air tubes and forty five burner holes, each about 0.050 in diameter. So do your bit of arithmetic based upon burner holes drilled No.60 (0.040 in) as these can be reamed out a little when "tuning" the burner. The shape of the box does not seem to be critical. I have made long narrow ones, shorter wide ones, and circular ones, all quite successful. The box need not be more than 3/16in deep and may be made from shim brass 0.010 to 0.015in thick. Put in plenty of air tubes. The whole lot, of course, has to be silver soldered.

The tank should be designed to a bursting pressure of at least 300p.s.i. For a diameter up to

1-1/4in. the metal for the shell can be shim brass 0.010 to 0.015in. thick with 0.015 to 0.020in. thick ends. I always press the ends in a simple punch and die in the bench vice so that I can ensure nice rounded corners to the flanges and slightly domed ends, which do not need staying. The tank must be silver soldered and should have a thickening piece where the bushes for the valves are to go - 'and when complete with valves must be hydraulically tested to at least 100psi. The nipple is drilled No. 80 (0.35mm) Much too big, hence the need for the needle to fill up the hole and to act as a control to set the size of flame required. By the way, it is as well to lap the thread on the needle so that it is smooth and does not tear the gland packing.

Threading both ends of the nipple enables it to have the mixing tube screwed on to it. If the lamp works properly upon first trial you are either a genius or lucky - or both. It is quite likely to burn with a smoky yellow flame far too high for the firebox. Screwing in the nipple needle will reduce the fuel supply so that the flames tend towards the desired blue colour.

What is wanted is a tiny, light blue cone from each burner hole and a purple haze of 'envelope' flame about half an inch over the little blue cones. If the flame still shows yellow when you have reduced the fuel supply at the nipple it may be that enough air is not going in because it cannot get out, so perhaps the little burner holes are a bit on the small side. Do not open them out more than about a No. 52 (1.6mm) drill; try drilling a few more holes to increase the total output area. Adjusting the reducing valve may help. When the burner seems all right on the bench you may find some further adjustment is needed to get it to burn properly under the boiler. You have to be prepared to experiment with these little burners; we are dealing with tiny quantities of fuel and adverse conditions in a constricted firebox.

The other type of burner, for fire tube boilers, is shown in the sketch. My example had a control valve operated by the boiler pressure and so needed pilot lights to re-ignite the main flames - and was

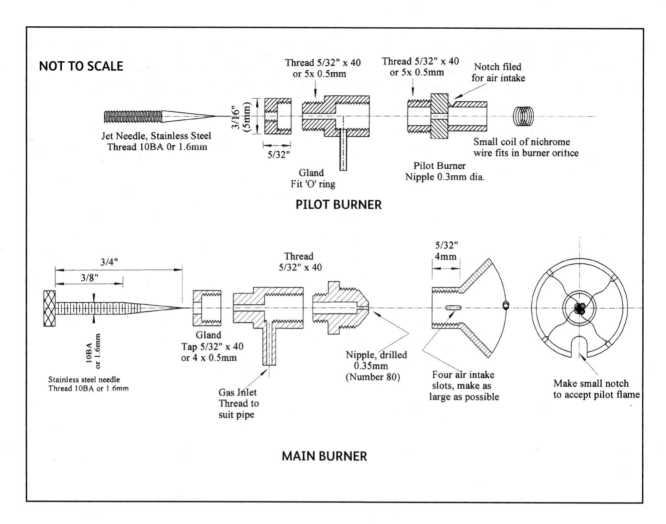

NOT TO SCALE

Thread 5/32" x 40 or 5x 0.5mm

Thread 5/32" x 40 or 5x 0.5mm

Notch filed for air intake

Jet Needle, Stainless Steel Thread 10BA 0r 1.6mm

3/16" (5mm)

5/32"

Gland Fit 'O' ring

Pilot Burner Nipple 0.3mm dia.

Small coil of nichrome wire fits in burner orifice

PILOT BURNER

3/4"

3/8"

Thread 5/32" x 40

5/32" 4mm

10BA or 1.6mm

Stainless steel needle Thread 10BA or 1.6mm

Gland Tap 5/32" x 40 or 4 x 0.5mm

Gas Inlet Thread to suit pipe

Nipple, drilled 0.35mm (Number 80)

Four air intake slots, make as large as possible

Make small notch to accept pilot flame

MAIN BURNER

A burner for use with Propane. Design by the late Don Gordon.

thus rather complicated. The sketch shows only the two burners (my boiler had two flues) and you will see that they are very short. Having virtually no mixing tube I had to put nichrome wire baffles in the path of the mixture to create turbulence and ensure mixing. These baffles are obviously a matter for trial and error, but once shuffled into the right place they seem to do the trick and result in a short ragged flame, which is fairly stable.

The boiler flues are plain tubes but in each one there is a "birds nest" knitted from nichrome wire, rather like an old-fashioned wicker shopping basket. The flame plays into the open end of the basket and raises it to a cheerful red heat, so that you have a bit of radiant fire inside the boiler. Much better than a simple flame; radiant heat does not go

round corners and up the funnel- it stays in the boiler where you want it".

Naturally since those words were written some more modern materials have come into use, for example the use of ceramic material as described when discussing spirit burners, has become quite commonplace, this gives a slight amount more heat than Don's nichrome Wire. It is however only of use with a flat burner and the torch type that ejects heat into heat tubes will still benefit from the insertion of wire into the tubes.

Making nipples might be a problem for some less experienced workers and this can be solved by purchasing a spare for an LPG cooking stove, this will not be threaded as suggested at each end and an alternative method of construction to that suggested by

Don Gordon will be needed. Drilling the tiny hole needs a great deal of care because few lathes will rotate at a high enough speed, the drill will therefore need to be constantly withdrawn to clear the swarf. Very small drills of suitable diameter can be purchased singly from good tool suppliers, note these are not DIY stores but specialist establishments, as a rule they are sold in lots of ten. Model engineering suppliers usually stock them in small sets of varying sizes in a plastic box. Modern tungsten drills in very small diameters are frequently available at exhibitions, usually sold by surplus dealers and although designed to be used at many thousandths revolutions per minute, with care and by constantly withdrawing the drill they can be used successfully. The drills are often available very cheaply on the surplus market and usually have enlarged shanks that enable them to be held in a normal drill chuck.

Anyone not wishing to make the nipple can buy one from camping shops where they are sold as spares for cooking stoves. It will be necessary to modify them for our purposes but at least the scary bit of drilling the hole will have been done, although the hole will be a little larger than necessary the nipples are still quite usable.

Tanks can be bought from a number of suppliers and will come complete with filler valve, home made tanks should be of brass or copper and assembled by silver soldering, soft solder is most inadvisable. All pipe work must be made from copper and fittings are preferably made of bronze, these too should be silver soldered where appropriate.

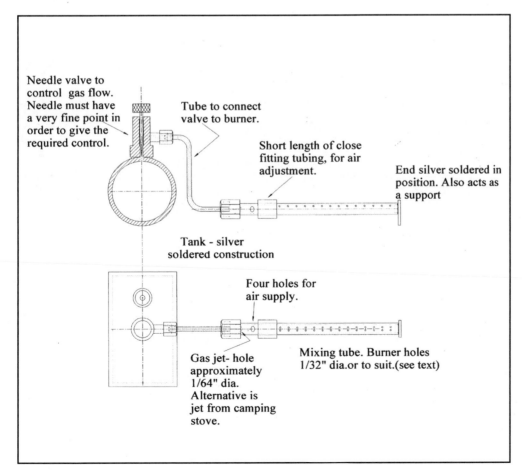

Needle valve to control gas flow. Needle must have a very fine point in order to give the required control.

Tube to connect valve to burner.

Short length of close fitting tubing, for air adjustment.

End silver soldered in position. Also acts as a support

Tank - silver soldered construction

Four holes for air supply.

Gas jet- hole approximately 1/64" dia. Alternative is jet from camping stove.

Mixing tube. Burner holes 1/32" dia.or to suit.(see text)

Simple LPG gas burner filled via a salvaged cigarette lighter valve. Primary air/gas mix is controlled by a Bunsen burner style sleeve.

Above:
Although not
recommended by
the manufacturers
many people
make adapters
and use small
readily obtainable
cylinders such as
this.Right: a small
gas torch that can
be used to heat a
horizontal boiler.

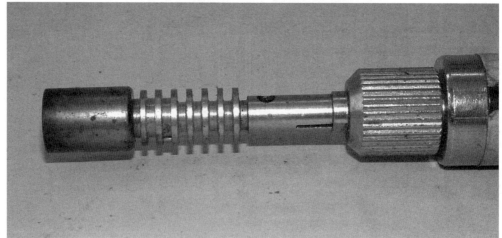

11
Boiler Feed Pumps

The quickest way to fill a boiler when starting an engine is to have a removable plug at the top and simply take that out and pour the water in, remembering of course to ensure the plug seals the boiler afterwards. Once the boiler is hot replenishing it is a different matter, the question of where the water might come from has already been dealt with and now we come to the method of introducing it into the boiler. Because the boiler still has pressure in it taking off the plug and refilling is out of the question. It is quite surprising how little pressure is needed to force the water out if a plug is undone and even a couple of pounds or so is sufficient to throw it with some force, and being hot anyone in the way is likely to get scalded or at the very least made extremely uncomfortable. Don't forget that the pressure as quoted is the figure above atmospheric pressure. Therefore wherever the water is taken from, it has to be pumped into the boiler, by means of a pump capable of overcoming the pressure, whatever it is, inside the boiler. It sounds a daunting task put like that but it is not really so as even the simplest of pumps will push the water out at a remarkably high pressure.

It is surprisingly how efficient small pumps are and yet all too often we see boats with pumps that are far larger than they need to be, many are made to designs that were intended for passenger hauling model locomotives, even the smallest of those will have a much larger boiler working at a considerably higher pressure than we require. In addition those pumps are usually only operated for part of the time the locomotive is operating, the rest of the time the supply they are pumping simply by-passes the boiler and is returned to the water tank.

The amount of water passing through the pump depends on the diameter of the ram and the length of

Mechanical pump operation is usually via an eccentric on the engine crankshaft.

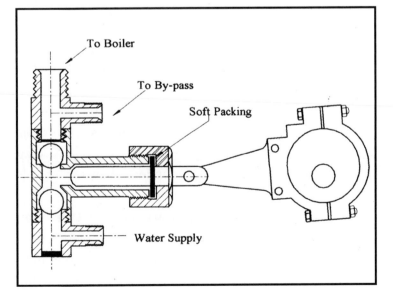

105

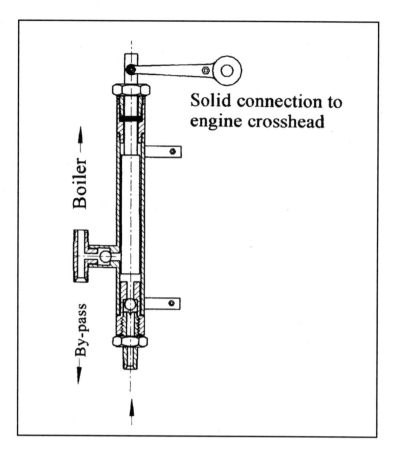

Solid connection to engine crosshead

Boiler →

← By-pass

A small bore and short stroke make the crosshead pump an easy and compact installation.

its stroke. A pump with ¼in diameter ram and a stroke of 1in is capable of maintaining a boiler 4in diameter and 10in length, the volume of that being at least 3 times that of the average model marine boiler. It is therefore quite possible to make a small unobtrusive pump that will be more than adequate for keeping the water supply to the required level.

Before considering how to make the actual pump let us first give a thought as to how to operate it. There are two types, hand and mechanical and ideally if the steam plant is to have pumps it should be fitted with both. The hand pump to be used when preparing the boat and the mechanical one to keep the boiler supplied when the boat is in operation. Having said that if it is not intended that a boat is to have an extended run there is only the need for a hand pump, and for those content to just fill the boiler and operate until that

is empty there is no need whatever to fit a pump at all.

Before going any further there is a safety factor that must be considered. Providing boilers are made in the way and to the designs described in this book they are perfectly safe, but they are only safe if used sensibly and with care. It is difficult to strike a balance between the time when the boiler runs out of water and the fuel is spent. Ideally the fuel should run out first and it is beholden on everyone building a boiler to take every possible precaution to get this right. But what happens if the boiler runs dry and the fuel is not spent? In fact nothing much at all, the boiler will get very hot, the engine of course won't work and any woodwork or paint near the boiler will get scorched. That is fine, but if a hand pump is fitted and it is given just one stroke, the pressure inside the boiler will shoot up to well over 200p.s.i.. It is the result of the rapid change of the water into a much larger volume of steam. It is particularly rapid because of the extra heat of the boiler. Providing an efficient safety valve has been fitted there will be no harm, the pressure will release with a loud noise and apart from frightening the life out of everyone, particularly the person who still has the pump handle in his or her hand, no real harm will be done. If the safety valve is not efficient the boiler could theoretically explode. It is more likely that the filler plugs or safety valve will be ripped out with considerable velocity. The author of this book has actually witnessed an incident of such a pressure build up although it was released via the safety valve on that occasion.

There are lessons to be learned from this the most important of which is to ensure the safety valve is in good working order. We tend to think of them as just a means of controlling the boiler pressure under normal conditions. In fact they are even more important for the sort of situation just described.

The main thing to remember is that should a boiler run dry, and the heat source is still in operation, never under any circumstances pump water into it, simply remove the heat source and go away and leave it to cool off.

The above is not meant to frighten anyone there is no need to be frightened by a boiler that is properly made. It is mentioned because the natural reaction, particularly with the water gauge showing empty is to put water in and it is something one just must not do.

We all know that a hand pump works by hand, but what about the mechanical one? Well basically it is a hand pump without the handle and the ram is pushed in and pulled out by a connection to the engine, instead of by hand The usual way is to put an eccentric sheave and strap on the crank shaft and use that to operate it, which is a perfectly satisfactory method of doing so. Another method is to connect the ram to the piston rod of the engine and allow that to operate it. If the engine is fitted with valve gear then the pump can be connected to the valve rod or crosshead, which are also perfectly satisfactory methods of driving it.

We tend to think of pumps as being reciprocating and having rams that push in and out and thus suck and blow water as they do so. Pumps using that method

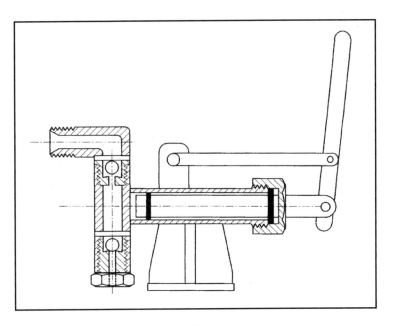

Typical hand pump layout.

have been in use for hundreds of years and have stood the test of time. What is not always realised is that a pump does not have to be reciprocating, the oscillating engine makes a very good pump indeed and it can sometimes be more convenient for use in a boat than the more conventional type of pump. For the newcomer to such matters it is far easier to make than the more familiar type. It should only be made as a single acting device and it is best to fit the piston, which now becomes the ram, with an '0' ring to prevent the pump from leaking water.

A typical hand pump, although this one was made from castings they are very easy to fabricate.

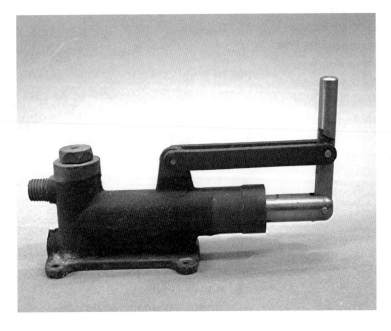

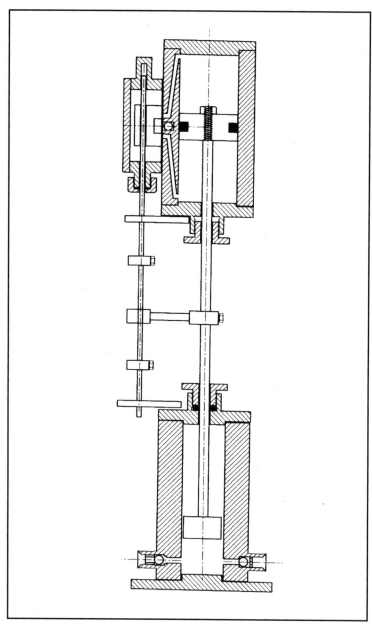

A simple and efficient design steam pump. The valve is operated by the cylinder connecting rod that connects directly to the pump piston.

Steam pumps

Small steam pumps are quite a practical solution in larger boats, but probably not so good in a smaller one. Making a very small one involves some quite delicate work, but if used such pumps have a number of advantages over the normal mechanical pump. The latter can only be used when the engine is operating, the steam pump can be used at any time that there is sufficient pressure in the boiler. It can be controlled independently of the engine and is very adaptable to radio control. In addition it is aesthetically pleasing to

look at and has a much more authentic appearance than the eccentric driven pump.

Injectors

The use of injectors for boiler feed is a subject that constantly comes up in conversation, in all probability that is as far as the subject has got. The idea is fine, as the injector is small and neat to look at and there is no doubting its efficiency. That is providing circumstances are right. Very briefly an injector works by using a jet of steam to give some cold water 'a kick up the backside'. This increases the velocity so that the water will overcome the boiler pressure and shoot into the boiler. It all sounds and is nice and simple but as far as model boats are concerned there are several objections to their use. Firstly, unless the injector happens to be a specially constructed one for use with hot water, the water used must be cold and cold water is not easy to come by on a model boat, it is unlikely that any carried on board will remain cold for long. It could of course be taken direct from a pond and on a cold day the temperature would be right. The objection is that the water is forced through very tiny orifices in order to give it the required velocity and no matter how well filtered it would be difficult to prevent these jets becoming clogged, no matter how fine the filter. In addition, although a really well made set up with an injector will pick up water from below its own level, as a rule the water is kept above the height of the injector so that it will be fed in by gravity, which rules out taking it from a pond anyway. Lifting water can be something of a hit and miss operation

Commercially produced kit of parts for an crankshaft eccentric driven feed pump.

and a sound not unlike singing. It takes very fine adjustment of both controls to get it right and doing this via a radio would be some achievement indeed. Finally when the injector first starts to work, a certain amount of water will be dribbling from the overflow and it requires very careful adjustment of the valve to stop this, without going too far and not allowing sufficient to flow. So unfortunately efficient as it may be in the right place, a model boat is not that and while possibly some individual somewhere or another may have been successful in using one, injectors are not at all suitable for average conditions or for anyone not well versed in their manufacture and operation.

Although both hand and mechanical pumps are frequently made from castings, they can just as easily be made from stock brass or bronze and the ram should be of stainless steel. The drawings show how to construct hand and mechanical pumps and measurements can be adapted to suit ones own requirements. The only proviso is that the size of the inlet and outlet balls that seal the passages should not necessarily be proportionally reduced, if they are made too small, they will not function properly The minimum size therefore should be 5/32in diameter for the balls with the passages having a minimum of 1/8in diameter. If it is possible to do so make them even a little larger than that say 3/16in diameter balls and 5/32in passages, but this will ultimately depend on the size of the pump. Remember too that a mechanical pump does not necessarily have to be horizontal; it can be made to fit any position or angle that is suitable.

By-pass valves

A mechanical pump should be made so that it will do just a little more than maintain the level of the water in the boiler, this then allows for any emergency that might arise. It is obvious that a pump that does this cannot then be allowed to operate continually, as the boiler would become over full. To prevent this a by-pass valve is used and it is designed to allow surplus water to return to

Hand operated water feed pumps are very simple to make and operate. Inlet and outlet variations can be seen here.

its place of origin, the valve is only really an ordinary stop valve, and can be either of the screw down or lever-operated variety. The advantage of the lever is that it can be adjusted by radio control, should that be necessary. Generally the valve can be adjusted by trial and error to a position where it will exactly maintain boiler level and there is then no need for further frequent adjustment. A little alteration will be required from time to time because as the engine starts to run more freely less steam will be needed and therefore less water as well. We are talking here of course of operating an engine many times before it does run more freely, so once the by-pass has been suitably adjusted the boat will have been used many more times before a change of setting becomes necessary.

12
Boiler Feed Pumps

Bearings

The bearing surfaces on any type of engine will need to have a regular drop of oil applied in order to maintain them in good condition and to allow free running. When first made all bearings are likely to be rather tight and although they will inevitably free up, if not lubricated, instead of just becoming free running they will rapidly wear. Heat from the engine causes any lubricant to dry out more quickly than is the case with something driven with an electric motor, so regular lubrication is one of the most essential factors when running steam engines. Light machine oil is the ideal lubricant for bearings, heavier oils tend to dry out and become very sticky when not used for a while and therefore take a little longer to become really fluid, so that there is an initial period when the lubricant is not really doing its job. This can sometimes create problems with an engine that will not give full power, because of the drag created by the oil. It will eventually thin out and become fluid but for places that are not near the heat of the engine this can take quite a while. Giving a good dose of light machine oil each time the engine is run will prevent these problems. The addition to the oil of a small amount of graphite is always beneficial, in addition to keeping the bearings free it also prevents wear.

Cleanliness

While a good supply of lubricant is essential do not over do it, there is little worse than seeing an engine that is absolutely swimming in oil. Apart from the fact that ones hands will inevitably get smothered in the stuff, which will then be transferred to other parts of the boat and spoil the appearance, oil picks up dirt and dust very easily and in no time at all the engine and possibly other parts of the boat as well will be in a right mess. Not only is it all very unsightly but it can also be a source of danger, should the oil happen to catch fire it will be very difficult to extinguish and remember that it is very dangerous to attempt to put out oil fires with water

Cylinder lubrication

When and how to lubricate the cylinders of an engine is something that is always open to debate. Because we are working at a comparatively low pressure, low that is in comparison with a steam locomotive, it also means a comparatively low temperature. As pressure rises so does temperature and

111

Commercially made lubricators, the one on the left has a valve on the steam pipe, this allows some adjustment of the amount of oil sent to the engine. Neither appear to have drain plugs although these are a desirable feature.

this means that unless a superheater is used, because steam condenses very quickly it will be quite wet and will itself act as a lubricant. Another factor to be taken into account is the type of engine employed. There is less need for continuous lubrication with an oscillating engine than there is with a slide valve and yet again the slide valve has less need for lubrication than a piston valve engine. Therefore let us look at the different factors involved.

Oscillating engines

If it is proposed to run an oscillating engine for short periods only, a squirt of any light oil where the port face joins the port block plus of course a touch on all the bearing surfaces, not forgetting the pivot will be enough to keep the engine in good condition. It also means that it will be possible to operate the boat without an oil separator, which will in turn mean less clutter inside the hull. If the engine is to be in use for long periods of time then it is worthwhile fitting a lubricator and no matter what type of engine is in use the lubricator should always be fitted to the main steam pipe, as close

as practical to the point where it will enter the cylinder.

Slide valves without a lubricator

In the case of both slide and piston valve engines a lubricator is advisable, however should there be any reason why fitting a lubricator is impractical, all is not lost. Drill and tap a hole in the steam chest cover in the case of a slide valve a screw cap can be fitted and prior to each running session the cap can be removed, a squirt of oil put in and the cap replaced. While ordinary machine oil is better than nothing, try if possible to use steam oil, which is thick gooey stuff that not only adheres to the working parts but also can help seal any minor leaks around the steam chest. It does not do that immediately but builds up gradually over a period of time, what happens is the oil around any minor weeps, congeals as it cools, thus becoming hard and creating a seal. This does not mean of course that a good joint should not be aimed for in the first place, it is just an incidental effect that is worth knowing about.

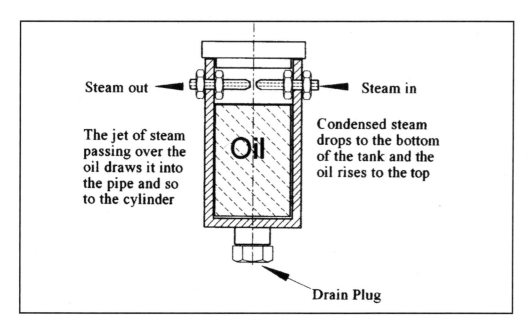

Steam out — Steam in

The jet of steam passing over the oil draws it into the pipe and so to the cylinder

Oil

Condensed steam drops to the bottom of the tank and the oil rises to the top

Drain Plug

Piston valve without a lubricator

For a piston valve engine a similar arrangement can be used except that the oil will have to be introduced prior to the valve, which means somewhere in the main steam line, as a close to the valve as possible. This might involve making a special fitting and although that sounds rather formidable, such a fitting need be little more than a piece of square bar with the screw cap in the side.

Lubricators

For any engine that will see more than light usage, a lubricator of one sort or another is necessary and there are basically two types to select from: the displacement type and the mechanical type where the engine drives a small pump that puts the oil into the cylinders. Both types can be purchased, although most that are on sale appear to be much larger than is necessary and they are best home made.

Displacement lubricators

This is a very simple device that is easy and quick to make. Steam passes over a reservoir of oil where a very small amount condenses and falls on the oil. The water being heavier drops to the bottom leaving the oil on top. The oil level therefore rises and reaches the level of the steam outlet and is pushed through into the steam pipe or steam chest. The lubricator consists of nothing more than a short length of tube sealed at one end, thus forming a reservoir, a cap is fitted on the top so that it can be filled easily and at the bottom is a drain plug. A small diameter steam pipe, with either a small hole in it, or alternatively in two sections, is passed across near the top and one side of the pipe is connected to the boiler, the other end going to the cylinder. The drain plug in the bottom of the body allows waste material, which is a mixture of water and oil, to be drained off. The unit can be constructed to a very small size making it quite unobtrusive and has the advantage of being very easy to build. Like all things there is a disadvantage as when steam is turned off, oil that is already in the pipe remains there and when steam is put back on it collects an additional amount, the result is a gulp of oil mixed with the exhaust. Providing a separator is being used this does not

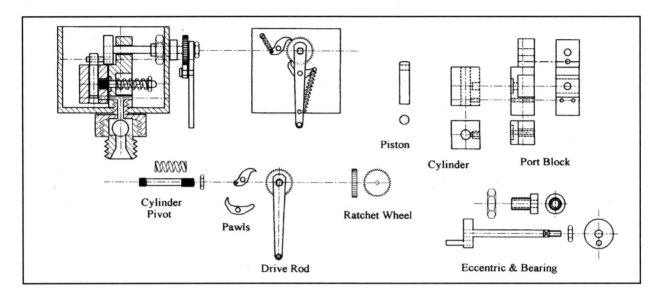

Piston

Cylinder

Port Block

Cylinder
Pivot

Pawls

Ratchet Wheel

Drive Rod

Eccentric & Bearing

matter, but without one this extra spurt will be ejected into the atmosphere. It is essential that the unit be made steam tight, in order to maintain the pressure to force the oil through.

Mechanical lubricators

There are two types of mechanical lubricator, the most common for many years consisted of a small oscillating cylinder in a tank of oil. The piston is operated by a disk type crank controlled by ratchet wheels, one of which is attached to the crank and moves with the reciprocating motion of the steam engine. A pawl fits into the teeth of the ratchet to prevent unwanted movement. Thus each stroke of the engine gives a single movement of one tooth of the ratchet and slowly operates the pump; contact with the ratchet wheel is maintained by the tension small springs. On large engines the pawl might be arranged to pass a multiple number of teeth in order to increase the oil supply to the engine. This is unlikely to be required on an engine in a boat. As it is pumped the oil passes through a non-return valve that prevents steam from entering the system. It is a simple but effective system.

Making the lubricator

Manufacture of the lubricator is quite straightforward, but because of the small parts involved some people do find a little difficulty with it. That apart anyone who has or can make an oscillating engine can make the lubricator. The cylinder is set in a small box and square brass tubing can be used for that, the top of the box must be removable so that the lubricator can be filled with oil. The ratchet wheel can be purchased from a model engineering supplier but is not difficult to make at home. It is made from silver steel and hardened. The pawl can be made from mild steel and case hardened but it is better to use Ground Flat Stock, or Gauge Plate as it is better known as that can be hardened right through.

An alternative design

The oscillating type of lubricator is very popular because it gives a good regulated supply of oil and is reasonably easy to make. Some people use a design with a cylinder with plunger type of ram. It is rather surprising that this design is not more popular as it to is easy to build and requires fewer parts than the oscillator. There is still the necessity to lock the piston at various degrees of its rotation and the ratchet and pawl is used for this. The oscillating pump requires the manufacture of a small stand to act as a port block and to support the cylinder, something that is unnecessary on the other type. Two methods of operating the ram are employed, the first uses a disk crank similar to that used in oscillating pumps and the second method uses a cam, the ram returning to the top of the stroke because of the action of a spring. Control is generally via a ratchet in the same way as the oscillating pump.

The latter type of lubricator has been in use for many years and some while ago the late Jim Ewins designed a modification. His design uses the same basic idea but efficiency is improved by fitting it with two 'O' rings, these eliminate the need for a non-return valve between the pump outlet and steam pipe. The design is still driven via a ratchet and pawl but uses a Scotch Crank, instead of the disk type.

Although the ratchet and pawl have been used successfully for many years they are one of the more difficult parts to manufacture and enterprising model engineers have come up with two alternatives. One is a clutch rather like a ball race that only acts in one direction and they can be obtained from model engineering suppliers and also from bearing suppliers, the other is the use of two small springs. The movement of the drive arm slightly unwinds these and when the tension is removed they spring back to their original positions. As they are fixed to the shaft the return movement rotates the shaft a degree or two.

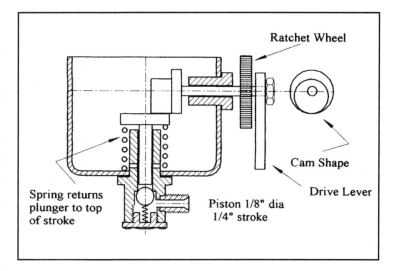

Oil separators

While lubrication of engine is essential it does create its own problems, as the oil that passes through the cylinders has to go somewhere after it has done its job and that somewhere is out through the exhaust. Being heavier than air once it has been thrown out, usually in an upward direction, it will fall back down again. It is quite possible that a quantity will land back on the boat and thus spoil the appearance of it; some will also fall into the pond where the boat is being used and pollute it. To prevent this a small separator tank should be fitted.

A separator tank is not a complicated item. It is just a small tank with two fittings, one to connect the exhaust pipe from the cylinders, the second for a pipe that will allow the exhaust to

This lubricator employs a cam operated plunger style pump.

These mechanical lubricators can either be driven directly from the crosshead or an eccentric or scotch crank.

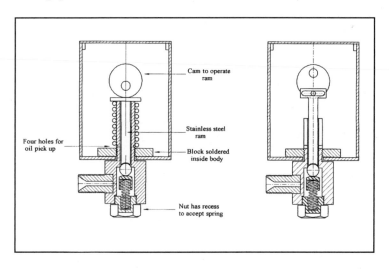

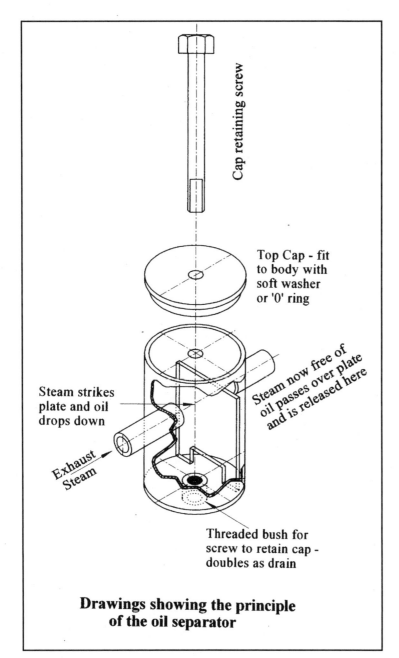

Cap retaining screw

Top Cap - fit to body with soft washer or 'O' ring

Steam strikes plate and oil drops down

Steam now free of oil passes over plate and is released here

Exhaust Steam

Threaded bush for screw to retain cap - doubles as drain

Drawings showing the principle of the oil separator

pass to air. Inside a piece of metal fits partially across the tank and the exhaust steam strikes that, causing the oil to drop to the bottom while the exhaust can continue on its way. The tank can be made to any form or shape that one wishes and small enough not to be obtrusive and spoil the appearance of the outfit. An engine even for a very extended period of operation will require no more than half a teaspoon of cylinder oil, therefore a separator able to accept a couple of teaspoons full of liquid should be more than adequate. A mixture of oil and water will collect at the bottom of the tank and a drain plug is used to get rid of it when operations have finished.

When carrying out general lubrication do not forget to put a touch of oil on the regulator in order to ensure that it operates easily, something that is particularly important when the boat is being controlled by radio in order to ensure that there is no danger of the regulator sticking in the open position. Similar attention should be given to pivots on valve gear if the engine is fitted with it.

Remember lubrication is essential for the efficient operation of a steam plant as well as to prevent unnecessary wear on the engine.

13
Going Astern

In order to reverse the boat, or go astern to use nautical parlance, it will be necessary to reverse the direction of rotation of the propeller(s) or paddles in the case of a paddle steamer and this can be done either by reversing the rotation of the engine, or using some other mechanical means to do so. The method chosen is of course a matter of choice but here are a few suggestions.

Changing the propeller(s) pitch

This is a method adopted for models that are driven by methods other than steam, such as internal combustion engines. It is also popular with owners of steamboats, where the engine itself is not reversible and a number of designs have been published giving details of how it can be done. Most of the designs involve blades mounted on pivots and a shaft that runs in a tube, designed to move up and down in such a way that it pushes or pulls little cams attached to the pivots. Not only does the idea allow the blades to be reversed but they can also be adjusted to change the pitch. The movement of the shaft controlling them is controlled by an arm that is usually connected to a radio-controlled servo. It is a popular method and is frequently seen in use.

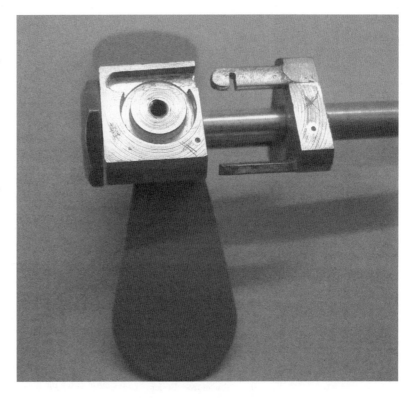

Reversing oscillating engines

An oscillating engine can be reversed easily by simply changing the direction of the steam flow. We have already seen how steam enters one port, pushes the piston down and as it returns the steam that is now the exhaust comes out of the other port. Put the steam into that port and the engine will run in the other direction and what was the inlet now becomes exhaust. There are various ideas on changing the direction of steam flow and drawings showing how it is done are included.

The working parts of a variable pitch propeller . The set up is based on a tube and as a rod is moved through it the centre section seen here rotates. The blades of the propeller have a pin that locates with the prongs on the outer tube.

117

The assembled variable pitch propeller.

fit then the problem becomes one of a valve gear that is so tight that it retards the engine, as well as being well nigh impossible to operate by radio control. Therefore if a valve gear is to be used, consider one that does not have too many moving parts, a selection of which are described in the following chapter. It is of course nice to make an engine that has the correct valve gear as it really looks the part and so the choice has to be made as to whether one is prepared to accept some loss of efficiency in the interest of authenticity.

Reversing with the valve gear

There is no reason why an engine should not be fitted with a suitable valve gear that will allow it to be reversed, details of some suitable types are given in the next chapter. It is inevitable that there will be some loss of motion in any valve gear, every pivot is a potential source of this. If they are made a tight

Gear boxes

The use of gearboxes for reversing has been popular for many years and details of working gearboxes published as long ago as 1910. Although no doubt the designs worked quite well they all suffered from the same problem of being large and very clumsy. Malcolm Beak, who has passed on so much information

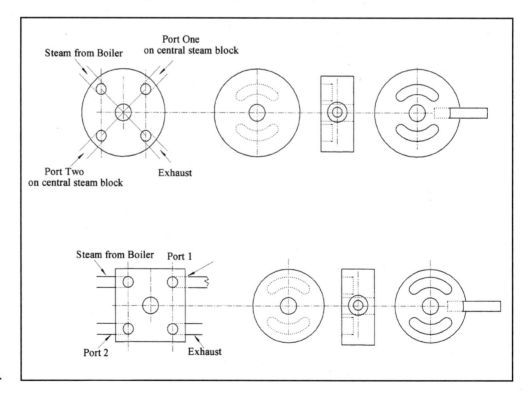

Usual type of reverser/regulator for oscillating engines can be made from round or square stock. The slots can be made straight to ease manufacture.

118

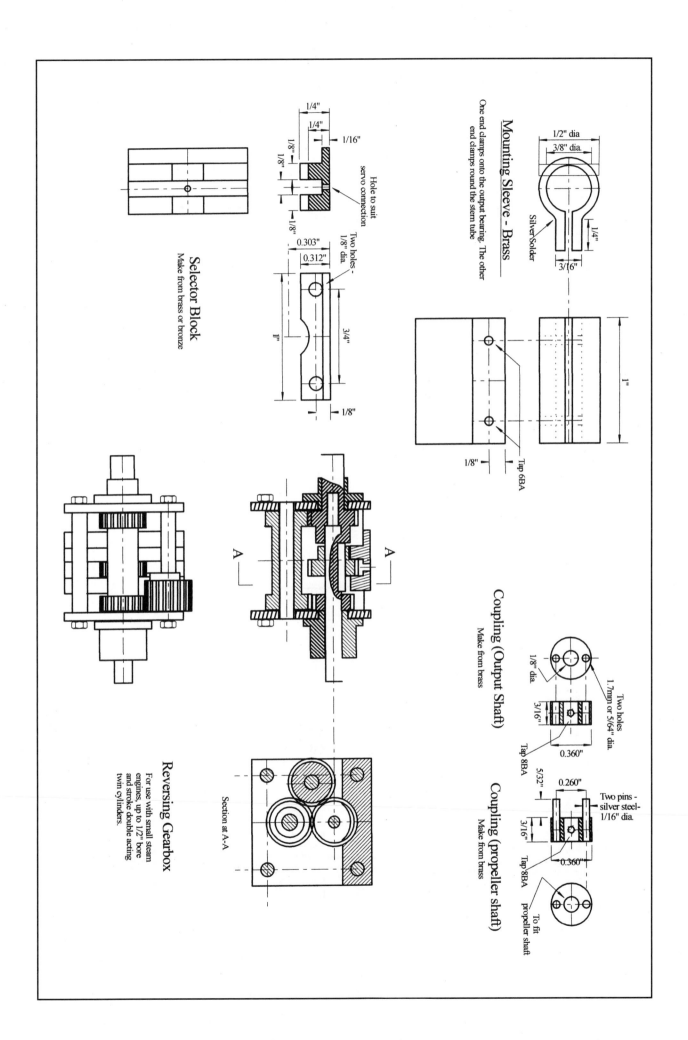

Mounting Sleeve - Brass

One end clamps onto the output bearing. The other end clamps round the stem tube.

1/2" dia
3/8" dia
Silver Solder
1/4"
3/16"

1"
1"
1"
1/8"
Tap 6BA

Selector Block

Make from brass or bronze

1/4"
1/4"
1/8"
1/8"
1/16"
1/8"
1/8"

Hole to suit servo connection

0.303"
0.312"
Two holes - 1/8" dia.
1"
3/4"
1/8"

Coupling (Output Shaft)

Make from brass

1/8" dia.
Two holes 1.7mm or 5/64" dia.
3/16"
Tap 8BA
0.360"

Coupling (propeller shaft)

Make from brass

5/32"
0.260"
Two pins - silver steel - 1/16" dia.
3/16"
Tap 8BA
0.360"
To fit propeller shaft

A
A

Reversing Gearbox

For use with small steam engines, up to 1/2" bore and stroke double acting twin cylinders.

Section at A-A

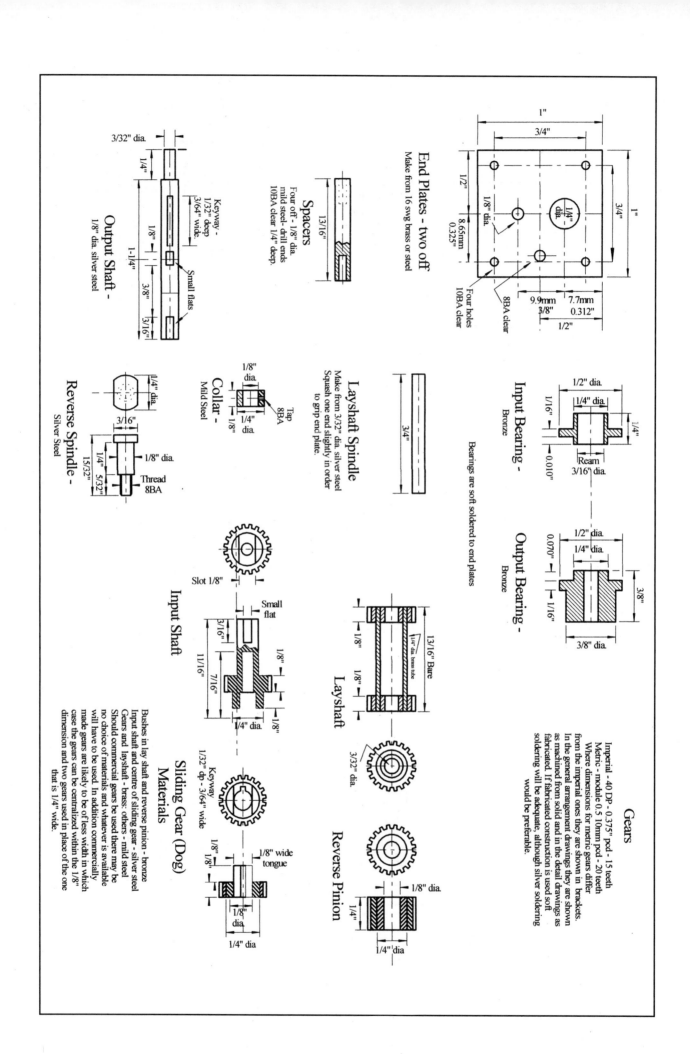

End Plates - two off
Make from 16 swg brass or steel

1"
3/4"
1/2"
3/4"
1"
1/8" dia.
8.65mm
0.325"
Four holes
10BA clear
8BA clear
9.9mm
3/8"
7.7mm
0.312"
1/2"
1/4" dia.

Spacers
Four off - 1/8" dia.
mild steel- drill ends
10BA clear 1/4" deep.
13/16"

Output Shaft -
1/8" dia. silver steel
3/32" dia.
1/4"
Keyway -
1/32" deep
3/64" wide.
Small flats
1/8"
3/8"
3/16"
1-1/4"

Reverse Spindle -
Silver Steel
1/4" dia.
3/16"
15/32"
1/4"
5/32"
1/8" dia.
Thread
8BA

Collar -
Mild Steel
1/8" dia.
Tap
8BA
1/4" dia.
1/8" dia.

Layshaft Spindle
Make from 3/32" dia. silver steel
Squash one end and slightly in order
to grip end plate.
3/4"

Bearings are soft soldered to end plates

Input Bearing -
Bronze
1/2" dia.
1/4" dia.
1/4"
1/16"
0.010"
Ream
3/16" dia.

Output Bearing -
Bronze
1/2" dia.
1/4" dia.
0.070"
3/8"
1/16"
3/8" dia.

Gears
Imperial - 40 DP - 0.375" pcd - 15 teeth
Metric - module 0.5 10mm pcd - 20 teeth
Where dimensions for metric gears differ
from the imperial ones they are shown in brackets.
In the general arrangement drawings they are shown
as machined from solid and in the detail drawings as
fabricated. If fabricated construction is used soft
soldering will be adequate, although silver soldering
would be preferable.

Input Shaft
Slot 1/8"
Small flat
3/16"
11/16"
7/16"
1/8" dia.
1/4" dia.
1/8"

Layshaft
1/8"
1/8"
13/16" Bare
1/4" dia. brass tube
3/32" dia.

Reverse Pinion
1/8" dia.
1/4"
1/4" dia

Sliding Gear (Dog)
Keyway
1/32" dp - 3/64" wide
1/8" wide
tongue
1/8"
1/8"
1/8"
dia.
1/4" dia

Materials
Bushes in lay shaft and reverse pinion - bronze
Input shaft and centre of sliding gear - silver steel
Gears and layshaft - brass; others - mild steel
Should commercial gears be used there may be
no choice of materials and whatever is available
will have to be used. In addition commercially
made gears are likely to be of less width in which
case the gears can be centralized within the 1/8"
dimension and two gears used in place of the one
that is 1/4" wide.

about his own experiments with steam engines, has perfected a very neat design that is quite unobtrusive and has kindly allowed full details to be published for the benefit of readers. The gearbox is a simplified and miniaturised version of the standard type that one might find in a motor car, but with only one forward gear, the drive gear meshes with gears fitted to a lay shaft and reverse is obtained via pinion meshed with one forward rotation to transfer that movement to reverse. Malcolm's drawings are on pages121-122

"Piston valve engines can be reversed by changing the admission of steam

Regulator

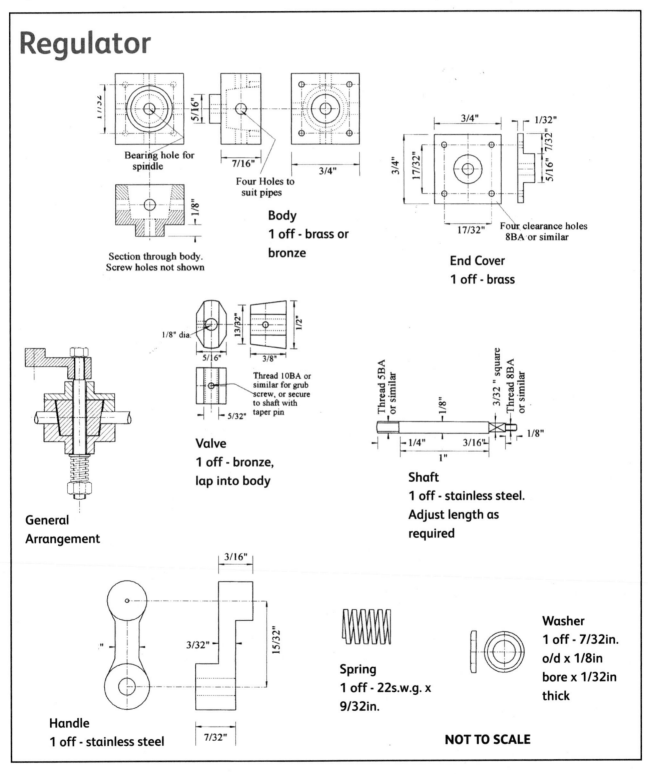

Bearing hole for spindle

7/16"

3/4"

Four Holes to suit pipes

Section through body.
Screw holes not shown

Body
1 off - brass or bronze

3/4"

17/32"

3/4"

17/32"

1/32"

7/32"

5/16"

Four clearance holes
8BA or similar

End Cover
1 off - brass

1/8" dia.

13/32"

1/2"

5/16"

3/8"

Thread 10BA or similar for grub screw, or secure to shaft with taper pin

5/32"

Valve
1 off - bronze,
lap into body

General Arrangement

Thread 5BA or similar

1/8"

3/32" square

Thread 8BA or similar

1/4"

3/16"

1/8"

1"

Shaft
1 off - stainless steel.
Adjust length as required

3/16"

3/32"

15/32"

7/32"

Handle
1 off - stainless steel

Spring
1 off - 22s.w.g. x 9/32in.

Washer
1 off - 7/32in.
o/d x 1/8in
bore x 1/32in
thick

NOT TO SCALE

Working principles of regulator/ reverser for oscillating engines.

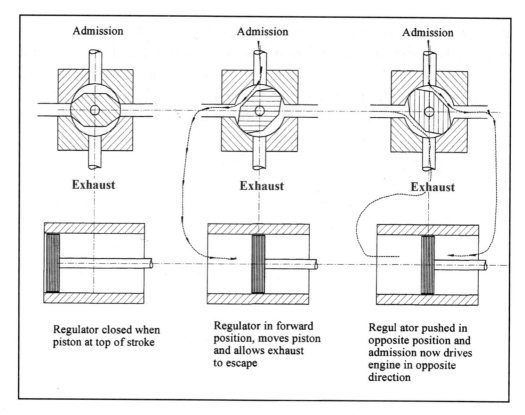

Admission · Admission · Admission

Exhaust · Exhaust · Exhaust

Regulator closed when piston at top of stroke

Regulator in forward position, moves piston and allows exhaust to escape

Regul ator pushed in opposite position and admission now drives engine in opposite direction

from outside the valve ends to inside and therefore allowing the exhaust to pass outside in a similar manner to that used with oscillating engines. It sounds much more complicated than it really is and while there always seems to be a tendency for piston valves to leak, the fact that reversing can be easily achieved makes them worth consideration.

Reversing oscillating engines and reversing piston valve engines by changing the position of the steam and exhaust flow will inevitably result in some slight loss of efficiency as unless the idea can be combined with some method of reducing the amount of steam entering the cylinder while at the same time increasing the flow of exhaust the steam will not expand as much as it should. No doubt this will be considered a small price to pay for an engine that will reverse easily".

14
Valve Gears

Valve gears are used to control the entry and exit of steam to the cylinders and are designed to get the best results for the conditions that are prevailing. In general terms this will mean that they will allow steam in at the right time and when it has done its work it will be allowed out. There is more than one right time for both these functions because by changing the time that the steam is admitted an engine can be run much more economically. Changing the length of travel of the valve does this and it is this part of the operation that the valve gear controls.

The effect of shortening the length of travel is to cut the steam off early. For example if we just put steam at full pressure into a cylinder and let it drive the piston back until it reaches the end of its stroke and then to exhaust, the engine will work perfectly well. But there has been no opportunity for the steam to expand and in more or less its original state it will be allowed out of the exhaust. This is bad management as steam engines work on the principle that steam is constantly expanding and that the expansion creates power. To look at it in simple terms: if we take an old fashioned a kettle, (not the modern electric ones that switch themselves off automatically when the water reaches boiling point), and with a little water in it heat it up, the first sign of change is vapour coming from the spout. Shortly after this the lid will begin to bounce up and down, because the steam inside the kettle is expanding and therefore creating pressure. In fact if the tiny drop of water was left to boil away, in no time at all it would fill the whole room. It is this that drives the engine and the valve gear is used to control the way the steam is used and does its work.

The remarkable amount of power that this expansion can create can be demonstrated by putting a thimbleful of water into one of the types of tin can that have a push on lid that fits into a lip, such as those in which treacle is frequently sold. With the tiny drop of water inside, push the lid on firmly and stand the tin on some bricks Light a candle underneath and then GET OUT OF THE WAY QUICKLY. In a matter of a few minutes the lid of the tin will blow off with a loud bang. This is the result of the expansion of the steam. *The experiment should only be tried out of doors, when nobody else is in the vicinity making sure that you are well out of the way when the lid comes off. Do not under any circumstances try the experiment with any other type of tin, particularly with a screw on type of lid.*

This gives some idea of the power from expanding steam, and so our cylinder that allows steam from the boiler to push the piston right to the point of exhaust is really very inefficient. All valve gears, whether

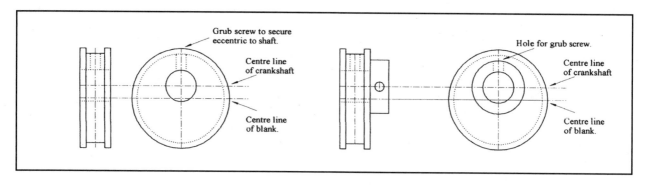

Grub screw to secure
eccentric to shaft.

Centre line
of crankshaft

Centre line
of blank.

Hole for grub screw.

Centre line
of crankshaft

Centre line
of blank.

Eccentrics can either be secured via a grub screw through the main body or in an extension boss.

simple or complicated are designed to cut off the steam in time for it to expand and do its work. The more complicated ones can be adjusted so that the time that the steam is cut off is altered according to the conditions in which the engine is working. The valve gear will, except in the case of the very simplest type, also enable the engine to travel in reverse rotation.

Altering the point of cut off is fine if we are looking for economy, or making an engine that will work in changing conditions. It is fair to say that with minor exceptions a model boat will normally work in similar conditions throughout the time it is sailing. Those conditions might vary from day to day, but it will not be by a great amount and so there is unlikely to be any need to change the position of the steam cut off. As a rule a boat working in normal conditions will only require valve gear in order to reverse the direction of rotation of the engine.

Nevertheless those who seek authenticity will wish to make the correct type of valve gear for their engine and in this chapter a number of possibilities are discussed. There are numerous valve gears that have been used with engines over the years, some are not suitable for marine work for one reason or another. Amongst the most popular with model makers are Slip Eccentric, Stephenson's and

Hackworth's; they work on different principles and will be discussed later. Right from the start it should be stated that in most cases due to the number of pivots involved and the fact that there will invariably be a certain amount of slop in each one, the use of any valve gear even if made most carefully, will result in a certain amount of lost motion.

Eccentrics

Leaving aside oscillating engines that work in an entirely different way to fixed cylinder engines, in most cases an eccentric or eccentrics will be used to give movement to the valve. In fact the heart of the valve gear is the eccentric or eccentrics and care taken when making them will pay dividends. There is nothing complicated about an eccentric, it is just a short length of round bar, with a hole that has been drilled off centre by a given amount. The distance off centre relates to the movement of the valve, so if for example the valve is required to move an overall distance of ¼in or 6mm, the hole in the eccentric is made 1/8in or 3mm off centre. Because of its rotation the actual throw is doubled to the required figure. Eccentrics are usually made from mild steel or cast iron, an exception to this rule possibly being in the case of slip eccentric valve gear, where instead of being fixed to the shaft

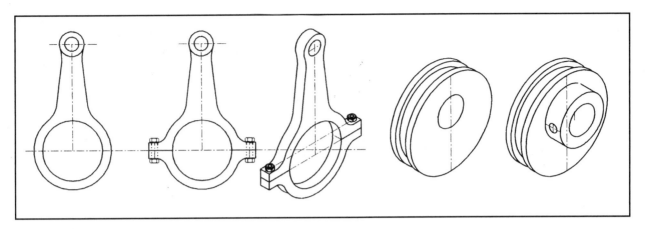

the eccentric is able to run free on it. A steel eccentric running on a steel shaft would soon cause a lot of wear and so in that case it is better to use bronze.

Eccentric strap

On the eccentric is a piece known as a strap and again it is not complicated. It is a piece of suitable material, with a hole to make it a running fit on the eccentric, it has an arm that is connected to the valve and the rotation of the eccentric pushes it in a lateral motion. It is essential that the strap is a good running fit on the eccentric; any slop will result in loss of valve movement and so impair the efficiency of the engine. It is usual to make the strap from brass or bronze, working on the principle that two bearing surfaces should be of dissimilar material in order to reduce wear. It follows therefore that should an eccentric be made of bronze the strap will need to be of steel, although if this is impractical brass could be used. Assuming that the more usual approach of using brass or bronze for the strap is used, then the bearing hole that will connect to the valve rod can simply be drilled.

Holding the strap in position

If the strap just rests on the rim of the eccentric, although to a certain extent

it will be held in line by the valve rod, this is far from satisfactory and so a means of physically holding it in position is required. There are several ways in which this can be done and the most obvious one is to put a lip on each side of the eccentric and allow the strap to ride between these. An alternative that is frequently used is to use a single rim or lip, the eccentric is then located close to a bearing and the strap is supported on one side by the bearing and on the other by the rim of the eccentric. This may sound a somewhat Heath Robinson set up but it is common practice and works well, it must be remembered that the valve rod will in itself help to keep the strap running on the eccentric. A third alternative and one that is frequently

Eccentric straps; left is a plain strap; centre shows the split style and to the right an isometric view of the split type with isometric views of plain and boseed eccentrics.

The eccentric below left has a raised section along the centre that mates with a groove in the strap to centralise. If the eccentric runs close to a bearing, only a single retaining lip is needed.

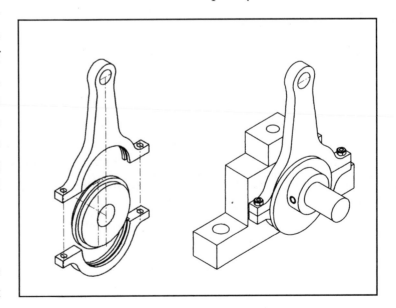

125

used on locomotives and traction engines is to put a raised section in the centre of the eccentric that will locate with a groove in the eccentric strap.

No doubt by now readers will be saying to themselves, "Hang on a minute how can the strap be put on to an eccentric with a rim on either side or a raised section in the middle?" It is possible to make a simple assembly with a single rim but not obviously so in the other instances. The answer is to slice the strap in half and then bolt it together again after it has been put on the eccentric. This is not as difficult as it may sound and to do so involves leaving a section where the bolts are to go and drilling and tapping for them before any attempt is made to bore the strap. Cut through midway and separate the two parts, bolt them back together after having very carefully removed any burrs, and then making sure that the join acts as a centre line, bore the hole, the strap can then be parted and rejoined after fitting to the eccentric.

Well that is the correct way to go about things when making eccentrics and straps, but not everyone is too sure about being able to get the cut line accurately or to bore the strap centrally afterwards. While it probably would not be considered good engineering practice, there is an alternative that does not require the strap to be parted or a rim or rims to be machined on the eccentric, the strap as suggested is made in one piece, and the eccentric machined to size. Two plates are then made that will bolt on the sides of the eccentric, effectively creating lips, without the bother of machining. The side plates, or perhaps we might call them eccentric edges should be held in place using countersunk screws, although there is no objection to the sides being riveted as long as it is unlikely that the parts will need separating at a later date.

It is usual to hold an eccentric in place on the crankshaft with a grub screw that can be fitted either through the rim, or alternatively in a small section machined at the side of the eccentric. Either way works well, but if the screw is put through the rim, then take extra care that the top

of it is below the rim. A small flat section can be filed or milled on the shaft, for it to grip on. Really instead of a grub screw the eccentric should be pinned in place, so there is no danger of it slipping and as a rule this is done with a taper pin. If for any reason, the eccentric is not set in the correct place and it has been pinned it becomes difficult to relocate it, so unless you happen to be really sure of your ability to set the eccentric precisely, stick to the grub screw. It is essential to lubricate the running surfaces of the eccentric and strap well at all times.

Valve gear advantages and disadvantages

A single eccentric connected directly to each valve will operate the valve just fine. It is only necessary to ensure that the hole in it is placed at the correct distance off centre for the valve events to be perfectly accurate, but if built in this way, the engine will not be reversible, unless the eccentric itself can be moved to another position. It will also not be possible to change the movement of the valve, although this is hardly important on a model boat. Whether or not to use a single eccentric depends therefore on how much control one wants and whether or not alternative methods of reversing the direction of rotation of the engine are being used. As will be explained in due course it is possible to reverse the rotation of the final drive quite efficiently by other means. Using the correct valve gear gives a finished and scale appearance to an engine and some people will prefer to use it to reverse the drive because they consider it to be more appropriate than other methods.

The slip eccentric

Possibly the simplest form of reversing valve gear and no doubt because of this has certainly found its uses in full size practice as well as with the model maker. Unlike more complicated valve gears it is not possible to vary the position of the valve and consists of nothing more than an eccentric, the details of which have already

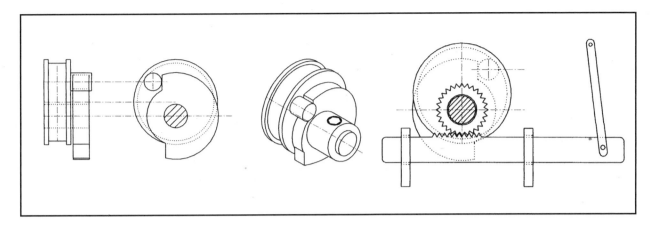

been discussed that instead of being fixed to the crankshaft it is allowed to run loose. Next to it is a piece that is concentric to and secured to the shaft and has a means of engaging and disengaging easily with the eccentric. Sometimes this will take the form of a cut out section, in other instances it will be a couple of pegs. The direction of rotation of the engine is governed by the relationship of the two parts. This means that the crankshaft of the engine must be physically moved in order to reverse the rotation, and while practical in full size it is not possible on a model boat in the middle of a lake. For this reason a slip eccentric is often considered not to be practical, while in fact it can be made to move remotely on the crankshaft and a number of methods of doing so have been used. The easiest of these is to fit a small gear wheel to the side of the eccentric and use a rod with a small number of matching teeth to rotate it. It sounds much more difficult than it really is and the drawing explains how the idea works, far better than any written explanation is capable of doing.

Single eccentric valve gear

The designer of the single eccentric valve gear is not known, but it is suspected that it was Henry Greenly, in many ways it follows the design of the Stephenson gear, using a curved link. The design only allows the engine to be reversed and makes no provision for varying the valve travel. Nevertheless it is not too difficult to make and has been used very successfully on miniature locomotives, so there is no reason why it should not be useful on a marine engine.

In the case of a valve gear that has two eccentrics, it is usual for one to be used for forward motion and the other for reverse. Both are set at different angles on the crank shaft, to reverse the engine the links are moved to a position where the second eccentric takes over thus changing the relative position of the valve in the valve chest.

The slip eccentric and the layout of a practical reversing system.

An isometric view of the practical slip eccentric reversing system.

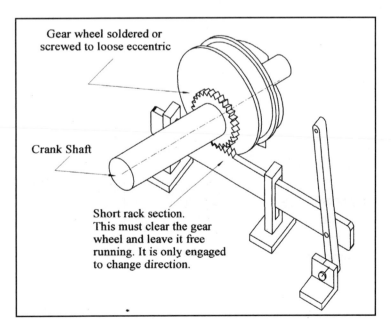

Gear wheel soldered or screwed to loose eccentric

Crank Shaft

Short rack section. This must clear the gear wheel and leave it free running. It is only engaged to change direction.

127

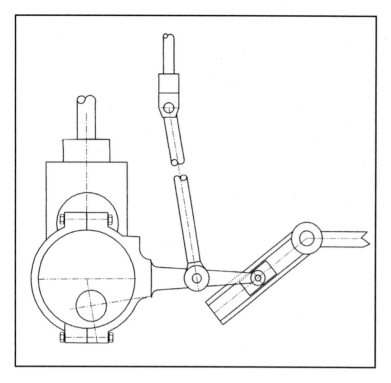

its function will not be out of place. It is a movable fabrication manufactured to accept what is known as the die block. The latter is moved to different positions on the link and this has the effect of changing the travel of the valve rod, which is indirectly connected to the die block. Most valve gears use a curved link, which is set to the radius of its distance from the centre of the eccentric drive. The fact that it is curved gives a more accurate and generally smoother operation than if a straight link is used, but the curved link is much more difficult to make than the straight one.

In fact the expansion link used with Hackworth Valve Gear is not at all like a normal expansion link, which generally has a slot in which the die block runs. In this case the slot is more often than not dispensed with and the link has two lips in which the die block runs, it is sometimes referred to as a slider, which is a very appropriate name. Some readers may therefore find the arrangement easier to make than a slotted link.

While the Hackworth gear has the advantage of simplicity, it was originally designed for an engine working in the horizontal position but can be adapted for engines that are of a vertical configuration. Because of the straight link it is a valve gear that is perfectly suited to miniaturisation and one that is to be highly recommended, particularly to anyone making and designing their first steam engine.

Hackworth valve gear is easy to make and quite reliable. A sliding arrangement is frequently used instead of the more usual slot.

Hackworth valve gear

This very popular valve gear was designed by John Hackworth and uses a straight expansion link rather than a curved one, making it rather easier to build. For the readers to whom the subject of steam valve gears is something of a mystery, perhaps an explanation of the expansion link and

Joy valve gear

Although in all probability the Joy valve gear was originally designed for use on locomotives it became very popular

Marshall valve gear is another easy gear to build. Lifting and lowering the eccentric strap on the single eccentric changes the valve position.

for use on marine engines. There are a number of variations of the design, but basically it is a very simple gear and requires little maintenance. The fact that it uses a very short expansion link, albeit curved, is a help to anyone who because of limited equipment is obliged to make the link with hand tools. Perhaps the biggest advantage of all is the fact that it does not need any eccentrics, it is operated straight from the connecting rod to the piston. It is necessary to use a thicker rod than usual in order to accommodate the connection for the valve gear and in full size practice a boss was cast on the rod for this reason. Because eccentrics are not used it is possible to make an engine using the valve gear smaller than would otherwise be the case.

Allan Straight Link gear

The Allan Straight Link Valve Gear uses two eccentrics and like the Hackworth has the advantage of using a straight expansion link. It is operated via a simple pivot arrangement but requires proportionally long eccentric rods in order to obtain full movement of the link. It is therefore only suitable for engines that have very short valve travel.

Stephenson's valve gear

This valve gear has stood the test of time and has been used in steam engines of all types. At first glance if one is not used to such things it looks very complicated but is not all that difficult. The hardest part is to obtain sufficient accuracy when shaping the curved link and in particular matching it with a curved die block of the same radius.

For anyone with a rotary table and milling machine both are fairly straightforward and it is also possible to do the job accurately using a vertical slide with a lathe, by making a simple device that will cut radii. For those without such facilities it will be a case of chain drilling then filing the link and hand filing the die block, it is getting the latter accurate that is most difficult

because it is so small. An easy way out of the situation is to dispense with the traditionally shaped die and instead to use a piece of round material, this will roll nicely along the slot and ride over any slight unevenness there may be. This should not of course be used as an excuse for sloppy work and the more accurately the curved slot is cut, the more accurate the valve events will be.

The normal advice is that both expansion link and die should be hardened, something that is not always practical and anyway the advice is intended for models that are used far more frequently than the average model boat. While high carbon steel like ground flat stock or gauge plate is desirable as it can be hardened, it is quite difficult to work with when using hand tools and so it is suggested that mild steel be substituted. If possible select a suitable quality and these days most model engineering suppliers stock different grades. It is tempting to use one of the free cutting steels such as EN1 but that would be inclined to wear fairly quickly and EN32 or a similar grade will be more suitable. If one so wishes the latter grade could be case hardened, EN1 does not case harden very well.

It is probably as well to make the die block from bronze as the combination of that and steel will give good running properties. Another material that has been used with success is nylon. When wear does occur, if a circular die block has been used, changing it is very easy something that is not so easy with a correctly shaped one.

Although there are numerous other types of valve gear that have been used successfully in full size practice, this does not mean that they will also be successful when applied to a model. For many years the Stephenson valve gear was by far the most common being to some extent superseded by rotary cam and poppet valve engines.

Poppet valves

A poppet valve engine is very efficient but making one in a small scale is not easy, it is very difficult to get the valves truly steam tight and the valve

Allen Straight Link valve gear is easy to make and maintain. The die-block is moved along a straight expansion link via movement of the valve and eccentric rods.

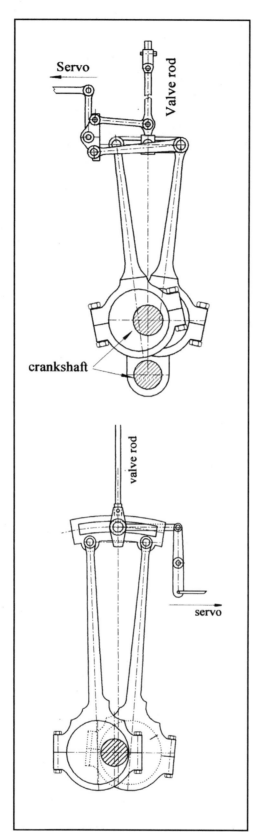

crankshaft

Stephenson valve gear is a popular and efficient system. The only difficulty in making it is getting the correct radius on the expansion link.

gear itself can be a problem. The valves as a rule are shaped similar to those in the engine of a motorcar, some people appear to have had success using valves with a flat face that are easier to make. Poppet valves are best suited to single acting engines, double acting ones can be difficult to adjust. The most common way of operating poppet valves on a double acting engine is to use cams and these should definitely be hardened as even a small amount of wear will quickly result in bad valve events.

Rotary cams have been around for many years and when properly designed are quite efficient, they are very difficult to make in small models and doing so is rather like watch making. Valve gears operated with rotary cams can be very efficient.

Make a model

The choice of valve gears, as readers can see is very wide and some can be difficult to make. A simple but useful idea before deciding on which will suit is to make cardboard models before starting. They should be made to scale, probably three or four times the required size. Pivots can be ordinary panel pins driven through at the appropriate places; the whole assembly can be put on a sheet of plywood or something similar. It is possible to alter the links until the required arrangement is found and then to use the design to build from. Making a model can save a lot of frustration at a later stage.

15
Turbines

While we tend to think of steam driven ships as outmoded and near enough obsolete, this is not true as many are still steam driven but instead of using the reciprocating engine use instead turbines. They no longer use old-fashioned boilers either, the modern ones are oil fired and as a rule will work automatically with little attention required. A number of countries power ships with steam generated by nuclear power. Nevertheless ultimately they are driven by a steam engine and this type of engine should not be ignored. The turbine is possibly the oldest mechanical machine in the world; a water mill is a turbine albeit powered by water rather than steam. The turbine is also one of the most up-to-date machines using gas as a power source it is used in aircraft, so it can be seen that the device has had a very long life.

Turbinia

The first ship to be powered by a turbine was appropriately named "Turbinia", it is a hundred feet long with a beam of nine feet and a draught of three feet. She has three inclined screw shafts each with three screws on each. There are three turbines in the series that worked at a maximum pressure of 170p.s.i., exhausting 1p.s.i. During trials the system was found to be very economical, in addition the machinery was lightweight and there

was an absence of vibration. It is then not surprising that from those early trials development of the turbine as a means of powering ships was quite rapid. Turbinia is now preserved at the Industrial Museum, Newcastle upon Tyne.

Like all machines the turbine has advantages and disadvantages, on the plus side is the fact that it will use steam from full pressure until that pressure has dropped to zero, so unlike the reciprocating engine there is no waste of energy. It is also very smooth running, with none of the alternating movement found in a more

Isometric drawing of the de Laval steam turbine.

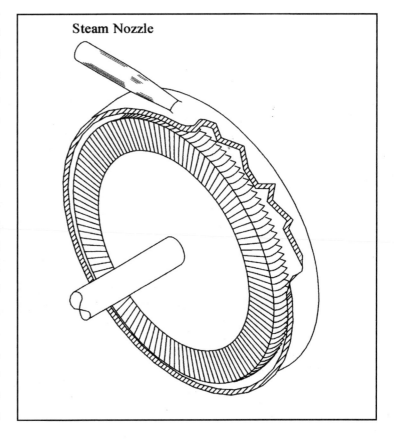

Steam Nozzle

conventional engine. Against it is the fact that all turbines revolve very fast and gearing is needed to get the rotational output to a reasonable level. Also most of the designs cannot be reversed and this has to be taken care of either with a gearing arrangement or as more often happens in full size practice, having a second engine made to work in a reverse direction.

A model boat driven by a steam turbine is a very rare sight indeed and yet the manufacture of a steam turbine is not necessarily beyond the ability of the average model engineer. The Victorians used to produce a model steam turbine, it consisted of nothing more than a boiler from which came a jet of steam directed on to the blades of what amounted to a fan causing it to rotate. Of course there is not a great deal of power in such a device but if that same, single bladed fan is put in a fairly close fitting tube, the power increases enormously. If we put a number of such fans in line on a single shaft to rotate in a tube then the power output is very good indeed. A catalogue of 1919 from Stevens's Model Dockyard, a company that sadly no longer exists, which specialised in the sale of model steam engines, advertised a model turbine with hollow vanes for sale as part of its normal range, the price was 10/6d or about 51p in today's money.

Basically this is what the turbine engine amounts to, a series of fans on a single shaft. Because of the expansion of the steam there are usually, but not always, two or three stages amounting a to larger tubes containing larger fans, thus making the most of the expansion properties of the steam. Here we come to another snag but one that it is not impossible to overcome. It is the fact that with all these mini-fans rotating at high speed they need to be well balanced, if they are not the whole assembly will shake itself to pieces.

There are several turbine designs and all are worth looking at with a view to making models and while some will be discussed, in this case it could be better to go it alone and use one's own design. Turbines used in full sized practice having become so complicated that it is impractical to follow a full sized design.

De Laval turbine

The impulse turbine as designed by M. de Laval in 1889 is a simple device, rotor blades are housed in a close fitting case and jets of steam directed on to them. The jets increase the velocity of the steam and this in turn pushes against specially shaped blades, causing the shaft on which they are mounted to rotate. The idea can be adapted to operate in stages, making full use of the steam. The blades are shaped to obtain efficiency, as with most turbines the shape is rather like a section of tubing and anyone wishing to build a model of the de Laval turbine could possibly use tubing for the blades, splitting it lengthways in order to get the correct shape. If the width of the saw used to split the tubing is taken into account the finished product is very close to the actual blades. As a rule the blades are quite short and are mounted on a heavy central section that acts rather like a flywheel. Because of the weight of the centre piece keeping the wheel balanced should not be a problem. The shaft as with all turbines should be set in either ball races or needle roller bearings, plain bearings are not suitable for such high-speed rotation.

Parson's turbine

In 1884 Charles Parsons also developed a turbine, it was known as a reaction type and in slightly modified form the design is still in use today. It differs considerably from the de Laval and has two types of blade. One type rotates on a spindle, as we would expect, the other is fixed to the outer casing, and the sweep of the blades is opposite to the moving ones. The principle is that having passed through the first set of rotating blades, the steam then works its way through the non-rotating ones, arriving back in a position to power the next rotating set. The cycle continues along the length of the turbine. The design is not too easy for the home workshop enthusiast

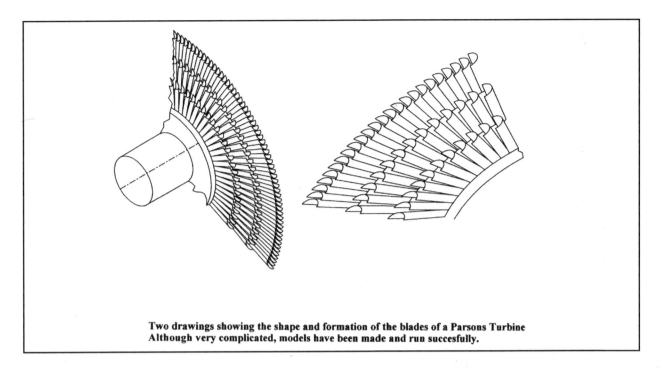

Two drawings showing the shape and formation of the blades of a Parsons Turbine
Although very complicated, models have been made and run succesfully.

to copy because of the fixed blades. It would be necessary to make the outer casing in two parts in order to install the fixed blades and would require very careful workmanship to get everything properly balanced.

Tessla Disk turbine

Entirely different to the previous two turbines is the Tessla Disk Turbine and it is also the only one that is reversible, changing the direction of the steam entry does this. It works on a series of rotating disks, separated with spacers. The disks are highly polished and the friction created by an injection of high-pressure steam causes them to rotate. The fact that the plates are mirror finished at first sounds a bit odd and the explanation usually given is to compare the surface to that of a golf ball. The shape of a golf ball has been developed over the years so that maximum efficiency through the air is obtained i.e. the golfer can hit it further. To obtain that efficiency it was discovered that dimpling the whole of the surface was best. Although the plates of the turbine

also need to travel at maximum speed in order to do so it is necessary that steam is able to get a grip on them. This will be best achieved with a very smooth surface and again a comparison can be made, if we lay a piece of metal on a sheet of wet paper and the metal has a smooth surface the paper will stick to it. Should that piece of metal be chequer plate or something similar the adhesion will be considerably less. So therefore the steam will stick to the smooth surface better than it will stick to an uneven one.

There are two jets, one for forward running the other for reverse. These have to be connected via a standard reverser as used with an oscillating engine, in order to direct the flow of steam. Whereas with the oscillator it is possible to allow the exhaust to come from a port of the same diameter as the steam inlet, because the jets used on the turbine are very small, this is not practical. What goes in must come out and so some form of relief hole or holes should be left in the end casing plate to allow spent steam to escape.

Shape and formation of the blades for a Parsons turbine are difficult to reproduce although successful models have been produced.

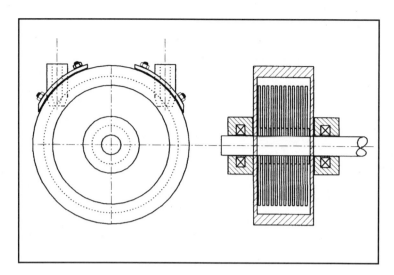

The Tesla turbine is the easiest type to build; there are no intricate parts but the discs used must be highly polished. Ideal for a warship model.

When the turbine is put in a boat, then obviously there must be some form of chimney to direct the steam into the atmosphere. To do this means that the jets must be connected to strike the first plate and a washer used to allow a gap behind that plate. The steam then follows the rotation of the discs and at the end of its movement will go behind the last disk and through the exhaust hole or port. Providing the jet is lined up correctly with the first plate it will not go behind that and exhaust through the wrong port. As the position of the exhaust ports will be largely a matter of personal choice, they are not shown on the drawing.

The Tessla turbine can be made to quite small dimensions and so is a very useful engine with which to power a boat. It requires steam at a higher pressure than the reciprocating engine, which means the material used for the boiler should be thicker. Parting off section of brass bar can make suitable disks, stainless steel would be preferable, but who wants to part off thick stainless steel disks one after the other. Whether stainless steel or brass, the disks will require polishing and everyone may have their own method of doing this. For the benefit of those who have not tried this sort of thing before, the best material to use in order to obtain a really high quality finish is diamantine, which is the material used by clockmakers to get that lovely finish on their masterpieces.

Turbines are fascinating engines and represent a challenge to the model maker, the finished result being worth the effort involved.

16
Paddle Steamers

It is now so many years since the paddle steamer in general service was phased out that we now tend to think of them only in terms of the pleasure steamers, some of which fortunately have been preserved. In fact before the invention of the screw propeller and with the general decline of sail, the paddle wheel was used extensively for all types of marine work and the use of paddle wheels lasted long enough for them to be driven by internal combustion engines. They have the advantage of being able to be used in shallow water where the screw propeller would not be practical and are still used in many parts of the world.

This ability to travel in shallow waters led to their regular use for clearing the fen drains and the small flat-bottomed boats were once a very common sight. This shallow water facility is also one reason why the stern wheelers were in use for so many years on the rivers of North America, where they were able to sail close to the river banks and pick up and set down passengers with little needed in the way of landing facilities. Paddle driven tugs were also a common sight on our rivers and estuaries where their manoeuvrability proved a great

Although as a rule this is the form we expect stern wheelers to take, they were at one time used in a whole host of situations for all sorts of tasks.

The Pleasure Steamer is how we generally think of paddle steamers and this is typical of the breed.

asset. Finally of course there were the ferries, most now superseded by large bridges, although some ferries still survive but alas no longer using paddle steamers.

Most of us will think of a paddle steamer as being a vessel with a single funnel, but there were many examples of sea going vessels with two funnels in line and also some ships had two funnels side by side. It is reasonable to assume in the absence of suitable records or any contradictory evidence, there would have been two boilers the funnels acting as the release flue for each. The boilers of course being positioned beside each other, it would have been a similar situation with two funnels in line, except that there may well have been multiple boilers as was the case in many large vessels. There is no reason why anyone wishing to do so should not follow these practices and use a system of multiple boilers.

Funnels were quite a feature on many ships, particularly the smaller ones. These often had to negotiate rivers with quite low bridges and the funnels were hinged so the whole thing could be put parallel to the deck while the ship went under the bridge. In some instances the funnel was lowered into the hull, instead of being laid flat. With the disappearance of sail the number of masts was kept to a minimum, frequently this meant just a single, comparatively short one near the bow, which could also be lowered in order for the ship to pass under low bridges.

It can be seen that there is a wealth of vessels worth modelling, and it is a great pity we do not see more models of them. One of the stumbling blocks seems to be the actual paddle wheels and yet these are not too difficult to make, particularly if modelling something like one of the old fen drain boats. The early paddles were little more than disks with a series of protrusions and little could be easier to make than that. More modern ships might have had wheels where the paddles were supported both sides, rather like a series of boards, between two hoops. More sophisticated vessels had paddles that feathered by means of an eccentric. Very early paddle steamers carried sails as well as being steam driven, sadly however the documenting of paddle steamers did not receive the attention it deserved. Details of the older ships are scarce and details of the workhorses, such as those used on the fens virtually non-existent.

This book of course is less concerned with the type of vessel than it is with the machinery with which to propel it and the types of engines used, were very varied indeed, so there are plenty of ideas for the modelmaker to pick from. For many years it was customary on models to use a large gear wheel connected to the paddle shaft, which in turn meshed with a smaller one on the crankshaft, this gave a good speed reduction and would also have resulted in some increase in power. It is an unsightly arrangement and if the engine is designed with reasonable care it is a quite unnecessary. The use of the method was almost certainly because of bad design of the oscillating engines that were generally used. The design of these and how to make them more efficient is discussed at length in Chapter 4 and providing the design of the engine is right the crankshaft can also be the shaft on which the paddles are set. As long ago as 1944 the late Henry Greenly, who was better known for his work with model locomotives published a very neat three-cylinder design of oscillating engine with which to drive paddle wheels.

It will be seen from the drawings that his design differs from the more

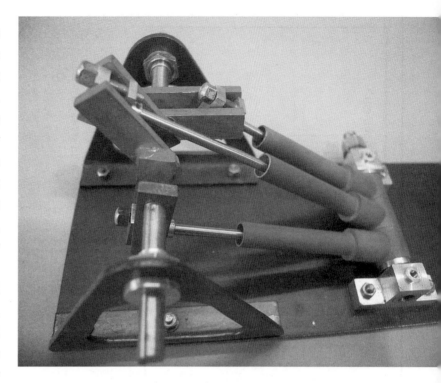

usual type of oscillating engine as the steam is passed through a shaft and via that to the cylinders. The result is an engine with a very long stroke, giving slow revolutions, which is exactly what is required. At the same time the design is quite compact and the measurements are easily changed to suit the requirements of a particular boat.

Not everyone will wish to use this particular design, preferring to use the more conventional method of making the engine, even so it is worth using the long stroke as it will allow easy starting and slow running.

A side on view of the fascinating paddle steamer engine designed by Henry Greenly.

The Greenly engine oscillates around passages in a shaft. The photograph shows the shaft with one cylinder housing removed leaving the steam passage exposed.

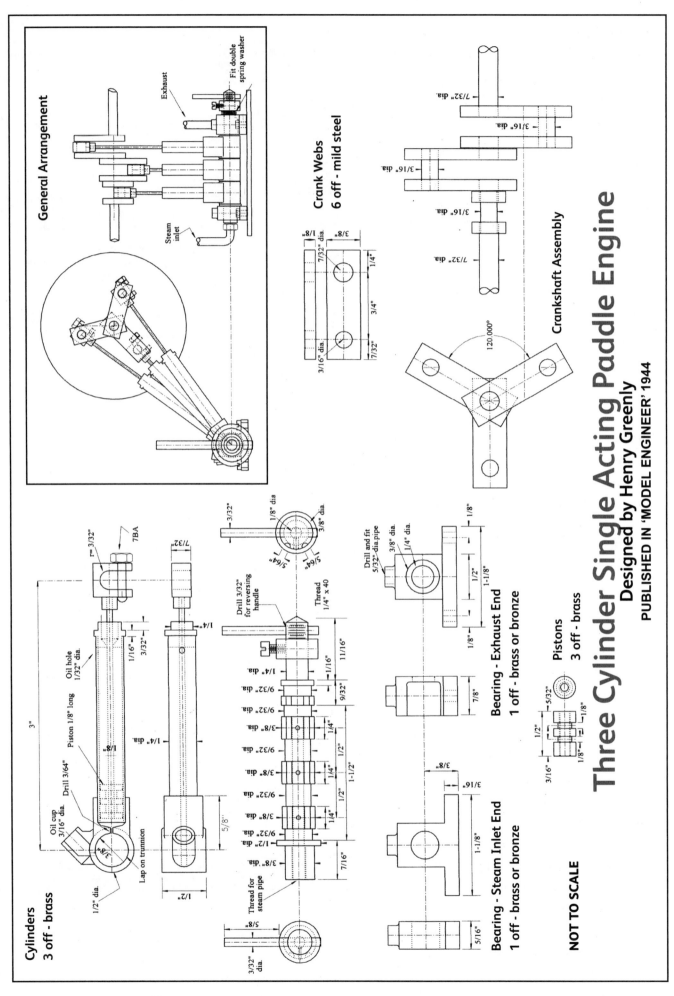

General Arrangement

Exhaust

Fit double spring washer

Steam inlet

Crank Webs
6 off - mild steel

Crankshaft Assembly

120.000°

Cylinders
3 off - brass

Oil hole 1/32" dia.

Piston 1/8" long

Oil cup 3/16" dia.

Drill 3/64"

Lap on trunnion

1/2" dia.

3"

1/16"
3/32"
1/4"
1/8"
5/8"
3/8"

7BA
r = 3/32"
7/32

Drill 3/32" for reversing handle

Thread 1/4" x 40

Thread for steam pipe

3/32"
1/8" dia.
3/8" dia.
5/64"
5/64"

11/16"
1/16"
9/32"
1/4" dia.
9/32" dia.
1/4"
3/8" dia.
9/32" dia.
1/2"
1-1/2"
1/4"
3/8" dia.
9/32" dia.
1/2"
1/4"
3/8" dia.
9/32" dia.
7/16"
3/8" dia.
1/2" dia.

3/32" dia.
5/8"

Bearing - Exhaust End
1 off - brass or bronze

Drill and fit 5/32" dia. pipe
3/8" dia.
1/4" dia.
1/8"
1/2"
1-1/8"
1/8"
7/8"

Bearing - Steam Inlet End
1 off - brass or bronze

3/8"
3/16"
1-1/8"
5/16"

Pistons
3 off - brass

5/32"
1/8"
1/8"
1/2"
1/8"
3/16"

NOT TO SCALE

Three Cylinder Single Acting Paddle Engine
Designed by Henry Greenly
PUBLISHED IN 'MODEL ENGINEER' 1944

138

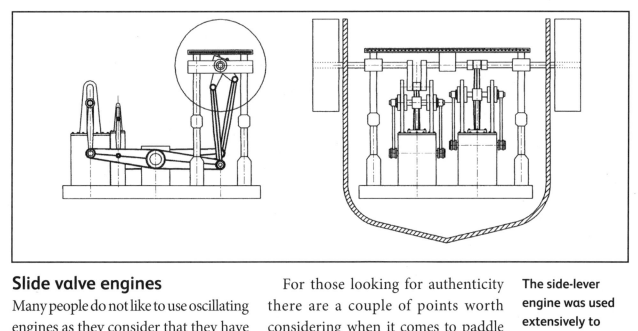

Slide valve engines

Many people do not like to use oscillating engines as they consider that they have a toy-like appearance and for those the slide valve is the obvious answer. Reversing is a bit of a problem in this case. In Chapter 14 reversing of slide valve engines is dealt with at some length and because of the considerable loss of motion with virtually all steam valve gears the idea of a small gear box is suggested, this is not a practical solution when driving paddle wheels. Slip eccentric gear can be adapted for use with some success and is probably the most efficient for the purpose.

For those looking for authenticity there are a couple of points worth considering when it comes to paddle steamer engines. While the oscillating engine was for many years the type most likely to be used, in later years compounds and triple expansion engines were also in use. Another type of engine that was used in considerable numbers was known as the side lever, designed with two connecting rods, on either side, for each cylinder, these were connected to the piston rod with a yoke.

The connection to the drive shaft or propeller or paddle, should also be something that can be quickly

The side-lever engine was used extensively to power paddle steamers and would make a fine model.

Seen at the Model Engineer Exhibition was this very fine paddle launch built by Martin Robinson, it is typical of a type of boat that was once to be seen frequently on our inland waters.

dismantled. There are several ways of arranging this with a propeller but it is a little more difficult when paddles are concerned. One way of doing so is to make separate spindles for each wheel and to connect than to the crankshaft with sleeves, using screws or pins to ensure they do not slip.

It is common practice for the engine in a model to involve a geared connection of the crank shaft to the drive shaft of the paddles. A small gear on the crankshaft, connects to a large one on the paddle and as well as providing a drive this also gives more torque and slower revolutions to the paddle. It is not something that is absolutely necessary but if the idea is used, laying out the gearing to mesh properly may present a problem. The best idea is to fit the engine on an adjustable frame and mesh the gears by putting a piece of tissue paper between the teeth. This will allow just sufficient clearance on the teeth for the gears to run freely.

The use of a thin drive belt on two pulleys is a good alternative to gears and is easier to construct. A number of materials suitable for making the belts are available and most model shops can supply something suitable, The material is usually joined by heating the ends and pushing them together, a miniature chain drive can also be considered. Suitable small chain and wheels are also available at model shops and less precision is required to assemble the chain and wheels than is involved when meshing gears. All three drive systems result in some loss of power through friction but this is probably not that important.

Stern wheelers

It is probably fair to say that when the subject of stern wheelers arises most people immediately think of the Mississippi Steam Boats that have been featured in many cinema films. In fact this type of vessel was and may still be used in many parts of the world, particularly in countries with wide shallow rivers where they provided a useful means of transport for both passengers and freight, some were also built specifically as tugs. There were even

some used in Great Britain in the early days of steam propulsion. The stern paddle wheel was also used for launches, some of which were used in Britain, although mainly they were to be found in America. The main disadvantage of these, was that because a very slow revolving engine was required it had to be made rather larger than the more usual type.

A common feature of the stern wheel was the use of hardwood bearings, and surprisingly these had a very long life, because they were well lubricated with the water. No doubt the fact that wood swells when wet also meant that the bearing remained tight and had an almost self-adjusting ability. The bearings, like the structural girders are things that would lend themselves to a steam powered model.

There were a number of advantages in using stern wheelers in shallow rivers, apart from their ability to be brought close to the bank, In the event of the boat grounding, something that happened quite frequently in wide shallow rivers, it was usually possible to move the mud away by rotating the paddles. There was a major structural problem in building such a ship as the weight and drag of the rear paddle, which overhung the stern caused some instability. The method chosen to counteract this was to put the boilers and fuel storage, (many boilers were wood fired) as far forward as possible. This in turn created another problem, as the boats invariably had a shallow draft, the hull was subject to bending. Using a lattice girder or girders to strengthen the hull cured this effect, the upper part of the girder acting as a support for the deck.

Needless to say there were numerous types, most built specifically to suit local conditions. Later stern wheelers were powered with diesel engines and are of no concern as far as this book is concerned. There were two types of paddles, those that stretched across the whole stern and those that were set into a well. These were as a rule in two halves, effectively making a double wheel. This allowed one side to be put into reverse, while the other was driving forward, enabling the boat to turn in a very tight circle. The type of wheel

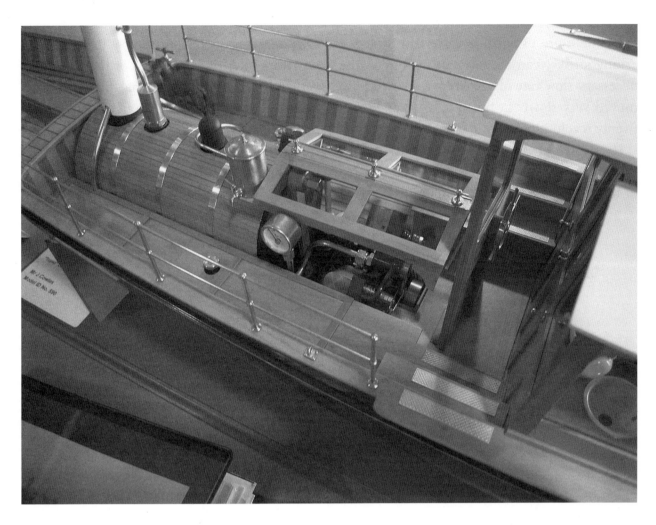

had a bearing on the engine that was used, or perhaps it was the other way round? However as far as model makers are concerned there are three types of engine that are worth consideration. The first of these is the grasshopper or walking beam, which was commonly used in pairs. One engine was placed on either side. Also used with this type of paddle was the side lever, which was popular with the builders of ordinary side-wheel steamers for a number of years. In the case of the stern wheeler the levers were horizontal, instead of at an angle as was usual with the more conventional paddle steamer.

Various forms of horizontal engines were also used and the wheel that did not go completely across the stern was usually powered in this way. A number of different types of valve

gears also seem to have been in use, the Marshall gear seemingly being the most common. For the model maker who wishes to keep things simple, the oscillating engine lends itself very well to the stern wheeler with an engine on either side as it will lay flat along the deck and be almost indistinguishable

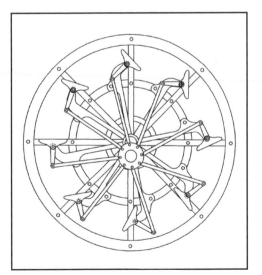

The steam plant of the paddle launch is covered with a hatch, which almost inevitable it would have been in full size. The photograph also shows the nicely lagged boiler and its fittings.

The feathering paddle wheel is popular with modellers. Not all paddle steamers utilised them, particularly those used on inland waterways had fixed floats on the wheels.

141

from the more usual slide valve and by using a long stroke, can be designed to run at the necessary slow rate of revolutions. The paddles moved very slowly in full size, often as low as twenty revolutions per minute.

It is difficult to establish a great deal of information about the wheels, some were capable of feathering, but there is reason to believe that early ones, and definitely a number that were used on rivers in Africa, were not of the feathering variety. It has been suggested that this was because there was a considerable amount of plant growth in the rivers which was inclined to foul up the feathering mechanism; the same reason the fen boats did not have feathering paddles.

17
Automatic Control

Having made the engine and boiler and connected them together, via a suitable regulator there is no reason why the boat cannot be sailed, either as a free running craft, or controlled by radio. Once the boiler has reached the desired pressure the regulator or throttle valve can be opened to give the required speed and away it will go. With careful planning the burner will maintain the exact pressure in the boiler and if a pump has been fitted it will have been adjusted to supply exactly the right amount of water, to keep the boiler at the required level, until such times as the fuel in the burner is exhausted. It is quite possible to arrange all this, by taking careful note of the boiler requirements during a number of runs, and learning exactly what adjustments are needed. Plenty of people do run boats in this fashion and thoroughly enjoy themselves.

Unfortunately no matter how carefully the adjustments are made it will not always work out quite as planned. For example, the quality of methylated spirits is very variable and this may well cause a drop or perhaps an increase in boiler pressure, this in turn can mean either more or less water is required and of course no allowance will have been made for that. The boat might sail into some choppy water, or against a strong headwind, which also requires that more power and possibly more water will be needed to replenish the boiler.

If the boat is radio-controlled then some adjustments should be possible, however it is virtually impossible to watch a small pressure gauge, when standing on the bank 20 yards or more away. The same applies to the water gauge, it cannot be seen and therefore it is impossible to know whether or not the boiler is running dangerously low on water. The device developed by the late Roy Amsbury and described in Chapter 9 goes some way towards solving this problem. There have been several other similar electronic gauges published in more recent times. These still have limitations, as it is very difficult to see the situation when

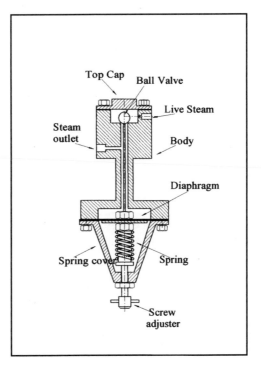

Pressure regulator designed by Chris Leggo will work with water, gas or steam.

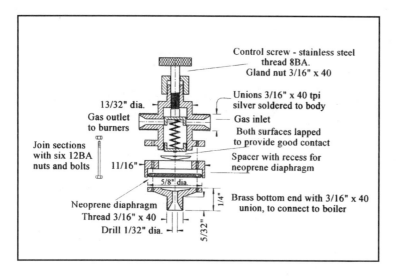

Control screw - stainless steel
thread 8BA.
Gland nut 3/16" x 40

13/32" dia.
Gas outlet
to burners

Unions 3/16" x 40 tpi
silver soldered to body

Gas inlet

Both surfaces lapped
to provide good contact

Join sections
with six 12BA
nuts and bolts

11/16"

Spacer with recess for
neoprene diaphragm

5/8" dia.

1/4"

Neoprene diaphragm
Thread 3/16" x 40
Drill 1/32" dia.

5/32"

Brass bottom end with 3/16" x 40
union, to connect to boiler

Pressure control valve for a gas tank designed by Don Gordon.

the boat is a long distance away, or is sailing in bright sunshine.

A more satisfactory idea is to fit a pressure regulator, or regulators that will automatically control, steam pressure, water levels, etc. Making these is not as difficult as one would think. They can be made very tiny and if required fitted out of sight as they can be rigged up to be quite remote.

If we take as an example a design by Chris Leggo from the USA published some years back it can be seen that it is a very straightforward machining job and can be made of brass. It consists of three main parts, the body, spring cover and top cap, sandwiched between the body and spring cover is a diaphragm made of neoprene. Steam enters at the top where there is a ball valve, a spindle is supported on the neoprene, underneath which is a spring, the tension of which can be adjusted with a screw in the bottom of the spring cover.

To explain how the device works steam is used as an example but it will work also with water, air or gas. Steam enters at the top and if the adjuster screw were to be screwed right out the spring would be slack and so the ball valve would immediately close and no

steam would be able to pass through. If the adjuster is tightened a little the ball will be lifted until the steam pressure on the diaphragm is equal to the force in the spring, causing the ball to close again but in this case the steam in the chamber is at the pressure dictated by the power of the spring. In other words a pressure known to the operator. If the steam valve to the engine, which is connected to the outlet is opened, the effect is to release the pressure on the diaphragm, causing the valve to open sufficiently to allow in more steam that is again cut off automatically by the ball valve. The system repeats itself, thus maintaining a steady pressure. By using it to operate suitable valves the water level, pressure level and gas flow can all be made self-regulating.

The late Don Gordon also experimented at length with automatic control of gas and produced a regulator similar in many ways to that of Chris Leggo except that he designed it purely for gas control and the controlling force is the boiler pressure. Assuming the boat has been fitted with a water pump that is driven by the engine, in the event of the engine stalling for some reason and therefore the pump too becoming inactive, this would cause the boiler pressure to rise and the gas regulator would close down the gas, ensuring that things did not get out of hand and the pressure rise to an unsafe figure.

Malcolm Beak has also experimented successfully with automatic control and made a successful unit, for which we produce the drawings, so it can be seen that there is plenty of choice.

For those who prefer to use an electric pump commercial units

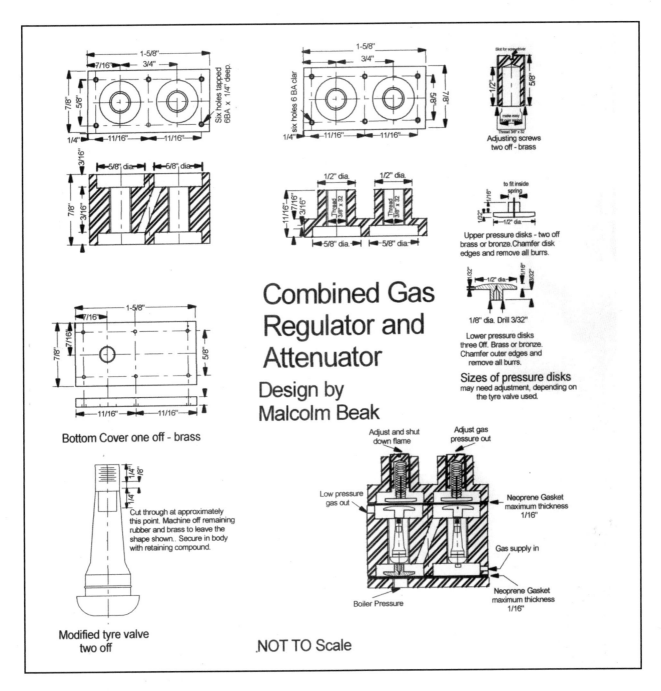

Six holes tapped 6BA x 1/4" deep.

1-5/8"
7/16"
3/4"
7/8"
5/8"
1/4"
11/16"
11/16"

1-5/8"
3/4"
six holes 6 BA clear
5/8"
7/8"
1/4"
11/16"
11/16"

Slot for screwdriver
1/2"
5/8"
make easy
Thread 3/8" x 32
Adjusting screws
two off - brass

5/8" dia.   5/8" dia.
3/16"
7/8"
3/16"

1/2" dia.   1/2" dia.
11/16"
7/16"
Thread 3/8" x 32   Thread 3/8" x 32
5/8" dia.   5/8" dia.

to fit inside spring
1/16"
1/32"
1/2" dia.
Upper pressure disks - two off brass or bronze. Chamfer disk edges and remove all burrs.

1/32"
1/16"
1/2" dia.
3/32"
1/8" dia. Drill 3/32"
Lower pressure disks three 0ff. Brass or bronze. Chamfer outer edges and remove all burrs.

Sizes of pressure disks
may need adjustment, depending on the tyre valve used.

Combined Gas Regulator and Attenuator
Design by Malcolm Beak

1-5/8"
7/16"
7/16"
7/8"
5/8"
11/16"
11/16"
Bottom Cover one off - brass

1/4"
1/8"
1/4"
Cut through at approximately this point. Machine off remaining rubber and brass to leave the shape shown.. Secure in body with retaining compound.

Modified tyre valve
two off

Adjust and shut down flame
Adjust gas pressure out
Low pressure gas out
Neoprene Gasket maximum thickness 1/16"
Gas supply in
Boiler Pressure
Neoprene Gasket maximum thickness 1/16"

NOT TO Scale

are available and no doubt anyone with knowledge of electronics would find no great difficulty in devising a suitable circuit that could be used in conjunction with two probes of the type used by Roy Amsbury for his water gauge. The idea of automatic control of water and gas is something worth thinking about as apart from enabling the boat to have a longer running time it is also an aid to safety.

The dual valve unit below designed by Malcom Beak incorporates car tyre valves of which there are three different types. It may be necessary to modify the design if a different type to that shown is used.

In Conclusion

Model making is done as a form of mental relaxation and as any doctor will tell you, mentally relaxing is good for the health. Whether the model is easy to build or complicated therefore making it is a good thing to do and so worth doing. Different people require different levels of concentration in order to relax, so no matter at what level it is proposed to build there is one suitable for you.

A great deal will depend on how sophisticated the reader wishes the boat to be as to how deeply he or she will need to read into the various sections. Some will wish for nothing more than a small boat where one lights the blue touch paper and away it goes, to be chased to the other side of the boating lake, turned round and sent back again, with the operator chasing after it, or hopefully even getting there first. All doctors will agree that this is a very commendable way to operate the boat as it means the owner gets plenty of exercise. Of course the lazy ones can have a friend at the other side of the lake and get them to turn the boat round, thus expending virtually no energy whatever and increasing the risk of getting heart disease.

Another person may wish for a boat that can be steered and by simply setting the rudder to the required angle, it will return to the owner at the point from whence it came. This is good mental relaxation as he or she must think about the correct angle at which to set the rudder in order for it to return and so exercises the brain to a limited degree, the doctor would like that. However there can be a double health bonus in this type of model boating as rudder settings are notorious for being unreliable, the boat therefore is unlikely very often to return to the operator, who has to chase after it, possibly at an even faster rate than the first person, as he or she is starting at a disadvantage. The result is not only a mental exercise but also a physical one, giving twice the health benefit and could even involve swimming which is also a recommended form of exercise.

The third person is the one who builds a very nice model and fits it with radio control, now they know the boat is going to return to them, providing they operate the controls properly. This involves continuous mental activity, so providing they eat lots of oily fish; to the delight of the doctor there is little danger of them developing a mental disease later in life. They certainly do not get a great deal of physical exercise but perhaps the additional weight of carrying the radio control equipment round will counteract that a little. There is one snag however, suppose the boiler should run out of water, or the heating arrangement of the boiler not work all that well when the boat is in the middle of the pond, performing the fancy manoeuvres as ordered by the radio. That will mean a big worry about how to get the boat and all that expensive radio equipment back again. This in turn will increase anxiety and that can even offset the value of the oily fish.

Finally we come to the 'Smart Alec' who not only has radio control but also automatic control of the level of the water in the boiler and the temperature of the heating supply. Well there is no worry about the boat not coming back, so there will be no mental strain and certainly no physical effort of chasing it around the pond. Therefore to the disgust of the doctor there will be no physical or mental effort. What does this mean? It means that he or she will have a lot of fun sailing their boat, and will possibly die younger than the other, but will have been very happy.

Why is all this in a technical book such as this? Because each type of modeller has been catered for and it is hoped that all readers will have a long and happy life, as a result of the information they have gained from reading the book.

The important thing of course is the pleasure obtained and it matters not which type of operation interests one. Just enjoy it and if this book has helped in any way to add to that enjoyment the author has fulfilled his purpose.